Forest Rain

*Spiritual Learnings
for a New Age*

Michael Forester

PEGASUS
HOUSE

First Published in Great Britain in 2017
By Pegasus House Publishing

www.michaelforester.co.uk
© Michael Forester 2017

ISBN: 978-0-9955248-3-5

Cover Design by Book Beaver
Cover Image © Michael Forester

Printed and bound in Great Britain by TJ International

For Komar,
with gratitude

By the same author

Books:
Dragonsong
If It Wasn't For That Dog
The Goblin Child *and other stories*

Poetry Chapbooks:
Love
Light
Peace
Forest Meditation

These books can be purchased at Michael
Forester's website: michaelforester.co.uk
To subscribe to the mailing list visit the web site

Contents

Foreword:
How this book came to be written

It was in the Summer of the millennium year that I began to write from the heart. For almost twenty years, I had written of profit and capital, material gain and strategies. But until that fateful year, I had not known what it was to bow my head to the calling of life contract and karma. The sun froze before my eyes, my carefully structured existence then petrified and crumbled to dust. I watched, incapable of acting to prevent it. I had nowhere to go then, but into the printed word. From that August on wards, I poured the substance of my energy onto the page.

I wrote, even in those days, of spirituality, as I groped blindly in my own quest for understanding and the heart touches of the soul. Many of the pieces I created rose spontaneously from somewhere outside myself. There were times when all I needed to do was reach beyond the dilapidated boundaries of my soul into the grain fields of eternal lore, in order to harvest ears of shining revelation. I knew, even then, that what I wrote was not wholly my own work – not in the traditional sense, anyway. Sometimes, I would feel the presence of a muse opening up my awareness and urging me to express what he wanted to say. I originally named him Cogitatis (Latin for "you think"), and when he came to me, I would wait in excitement, holding my breath until he spoke. Then, my fingers would fly across the keyboard, as I articulated and paraphrased the wisdom he initiated.

It was not until December 2001, though, that I began to be aware of my calling. My quest for spiritual awareness had taken me to a small group of people that met just outside Southampton, UK. There, I met a psychic. When I spoke of my passion for writing, she called me aside, and asked if I wrote spiritually, for she had been told that this was my vocation and that I had an old soul working with me. Evidently, what I had felt concerning the muse was in some sense accurate. Fascinated, I took the psychic's address and telephone number with a view to meeting her in order to discuss the matter more fully. I then, promptly lost the details!

I came close to drowning in the waves of turbulence that surrounded me that month. As I was thrown uncontrollably between a future I thought I wanted and one that I believed deep down to be inevitable, the pendulum of my reality oscillated faster and faster. It was more than my conscious mind could bear. Pushed beyond my limit, I took an intended fatal drug overdose on New Year's Day 2002, and abandoned myself to whatever fate lay thereafter. At that point, it seemed to me that any possibility, from ceasing to exist to spending eternity in Hell was preferable to what I was experiencing at that moment.

I was unconscious for six hours before they found me. By all medical rights, I should have died. I wondered long and deep as to what happened during those hours. Though I had no conscious recollection, something in me witnessed that there were significant events afoot; that I had negotiated at heaven's gate and finally, accepted that I had to return, in order to see the pain through, and gain the learning necessary to this lifetime. The speed of my recovery bears witness to the uncommonness of the circumstances, for I was out of hospital two days later. It was not until June that I was to be granted an understanding of what had actually happened to me that day. A lot more had been at stake than I had realised.

From that time forward, there commenced the most intense period of spiritual awareness and revelation that I have ever experienced in this lifetime. Six months on, at the time of writing, it continues unabated.

Five days after the turn of the year, I was driving to visit a friend. During the journey, as my thoughts wandered, a phrase appeared in my mind without warning: "Feed my sheep." I was confused, momentarily, not recalling its origin. Then, the memory rose from way back in my personal history. They were the words spoken by Jesus to Simon Peter after the betrayal.

"Simon Peter, do you love me?"

"Yes, Lord, you know that I am your friend."

"Feed my sheep"

The exchange is repeated three times until finally, Peter acknowledges his love for Jesus. Peter is overcome with Jesus' forgiveness and accepts in his heart his commission.

I thought no more of this until I returned home that evening and was relating the story to a friend on the telephone. It was then, that the enormity of the revelation struck me – that I had just received my own commission. I knew at the speed of thought, in the way that we can only know something revealed to us in unadulterated illumination, that I had just received my vocation for the rest of this life; that I was to write in order to feed the sheep.

Further confirmation followed. Two days later, I attended another group for the first time, "Hearts & Hands," which met in the village of Burley in Hampshire, UK. There, during a meditation, I felt the presence of a spirit – an event to which I am assuredly not prone! I asked, "Who are you?" and was stunned beyond my means to express when the answer came back "Jesus." I asked why I had not been permitted to come home on New Year's Day. The answer was "Because I have work for you to do." I had received the first confirmation of the calling.

The matter did not rest there though. At the same meeting, the Psychic who had first piqued my curiosity was present again. It was the only time she had ever attended that group. This time, I did not lose her address! Rather, I entered into a period of spiritual healing with her that was to last for four months. Gradually, the healer and my spirit guides channelled restorative energy into me, building up my reserves and returning me to health more rapidly than I would ever have conceived possible. During the healing sessions, a certain spirit began to appear to the healer in the form of an Aborigine. After one of the sessions, he spoke a message to me directly through her:

> *"Many Learnings come from you. Lot of wisdom lie deep in you, coming to the surface.*
>
> *You had to go through the deepest depths, so that you could cope no more; so that you had that lifeline thrown to you and you grabbed it.*
>
> *Many people need to hear these learnings. When the rope comes down, it is like a ladder. You had to climb up because*

the work is so important; had to go down low to reach the steps and climb up the ladder, that you would never reach the depths ever again; proof to you that your work is very important."

I had received the second confirmation of the calling.

As time passed, the Aborigine came to me more and more often, in due course, revealing himself to me as the "muse" I had become aware of, in the early days of my writing. He appeared to find the name Cogitatis highly amusing, and for some time, would not disclose his real name to me. Clearly, some spirit teachers have a sense of humour!

On 5th June 2002, my teacher revealed yet more to me of the importance of these writings or "Learnings", as he had termed them. He came to me during past life regression and showed me in detail what had transpired on 1st January, the day of my intended death. Now, revealing his true name as Komar, while I was deep in trance, he took me back to the time when I fell asleep through the action of the drugs I had taken.

Komar showed me he had been my teacher for a long, long time – through many lifetimes and beyond, whilst, we worked towards a task of great importance together. The Learnings that we were writing together, now, contained in this book and perhaps other books to follow, were too important to be delayed until I could incarnate again into another lifetime. They were needed now, and for this reason, if no other, I was not to end my life that day. Komar showed me that many people were awaiting the Learnings, both here and in the spirit world, for together, we were writing what he referred to as a "Life Book". I am still not fully clear as to the meaning of the term.

It was then, that he showed me his own commitment to me and to the work, for I understood that he had entered into my body with me that day. He gave me to understand that over a period of some hours, he combined his own energy with mine, to prevent the absorption of the drugs into my bloodstream and the damaging of my organs that would have resulted. When the process was completed and he knew I was safe, he communicated to a member of my family, who was many miles away, that there was something wrong with me and I needed help. As a result, another family member came to find me and woke me up, arranging for me to be taken to hospital. It was to be almost three months before I heard from Komar again. So depleted was his own energy from this selfless act of love, that he himself had gone away to regenerate.

A new life began for me that day, one founded on spiritual awareness and a fervent desire to grow spiritually. A cornerstone of my life remains, the Learnings that Komar brings – the kernels of wisdom that he bids me, nurture into living plants of luxuriant foliage through the use of language that is more mine than his.

I commend to you the "Many Learnings" that Komar brings, with the fervent wish that they will edify you and lead you towards the light that is the end of all journeys. For it seems to me that I have no serious option but to bring them to you. Quite simply, I have to touch your soul.

1. Am I a writer?

I'm asking because I really want to know. You see, there is a really special reason why I ask. Some day, soon, I'm going to tell you about it. It's really important to me. And I value your opinion so highly.

You have always touched my soul.

Let's be clear about things before we start. When I say I want to write, I don't mean, the kind of writing where you pick up a pen and explain things to people. If you want to know about residual interest or routes to India, if you're into baking bread or working wood, should you seek enlightenment by quantum physics or questioning psychics, I am not your man.

I want to touch your soul.

Please understand me. I will not… cannot, offer you polite conversation. We will not talk of the weather we've been having, or how mother is, with her bunions. I do not want to know of the colour of your carpets or the bulge in your bank account or with which new trinket you have sought to quench the unconscious thirst of your quest. I will have no truck with chaff. I'm not that kind of man. Do not walk or work with me because you are bored and have nothing better to do. I plan to be too demanding of you for that. Do not give me the fag ends of your time. Do not give me half your attention while you give the other half to the Simpsons and yet, a further half to the dinner heating in the microwave. I will touch you deep, or not at all.

I have to touch your soul.

Truth is, I need to know that I can move you, even as I am moved. I will sculpt in silence and draw images in the air; to weave tapestries in the Tao and slay sacrifices upon the altar of my own sensibilities. So, tell me, are my offerings, a sweet smelling savour to your senses? When I kill the fatted calves of my prejudice within your temple gates, am I redeemed? Are my sins covered? Am I acceptable to you? And, if acceptable, can I approach the holy of holies of your being and bidden, enter, sup with you?

I seek to touch your soul.

If I cannot raise you to heights of passionate indignation with my righteous anger... then, I am not a writer. If I cannot leave you outraged at my unreasoned prejudices... I am not a writer... If I cannot make you smile with glee or make you lose control with laughter until both our sides are aching... I am not a writer. If I cannot stir you to protect me when I am abused... I am not a writer. If I cannot move you to tears when my own tears soak your feet ... If I cannot make you cry in pain at the pain that stirs me, sweat-drenched from my sleep... I am not a writer. Do you understand that...

I need to touch your soul.

We will set out on a journey soon. We two, will travel side by side and grow oblivious of others on the road, lost in the depths of intimate conversation. I will show you my world and dare to hope that you will bid me explore yours. At the point of departure, we are, as yet, the merest acquaintances. So, just now...

it would not be safe to let me touch your soul.

You do not know me well enough – as yet. As we commence our pilgrimage, we both shall keep our sword hands free... each, ready to un-sheath steel, so as to protect ourselves from the other at a moment's notice... if need be. And yet, a while, we circle cautiously, eye on eye until we each are sure, the other is no threat. I promise, I will do no harm if you will....

please, let me touch your soul.

Be sure, you will know, you have been touched. But, I promise you that I will tread lightly on your heart. You have but one ... and the joy you hold therein, is precious to me. The pleasure and places you have known are of countless worth and the memories you hold shall not be treated with disdain. So, if, as you walk with me, we talk of use and abuse, I will not use you nor abuse you. We will speak of pain and passion... but I will not be the architect of pain or passion that you do not choose to feel. Only enough... barely enough... to let you know you live still. Only enough…. barely enough… to give you the building blocks you need today to add to the edifice you are constructing at the centre of your identity. And we will pause our pilgrimage today, in order to labour at that energising task together with passion and with joy; but only, if you consider the materials I supply to be of choicest richness for your construction. If I can add just a little to the temple you build daily in your spirit, it will be enough for me. I shall work conscientiously. Though I am but an apprentice, I shall make my workmanship adequate. And perhaps… if I have helped a little… one day, I shall be able to call myself "craftsman."

As we walk together, we will draw closer. The time may one day come when you need my help. Then, you will reach out for me and find me here, beside you. You will come to know me… perhaps, to know me intimately, as I open my heart to you. For…

I will let you touch my soul.

I ask you to tread lightly on my heart. I have but one… and there are only so many times I can afford to have it broken. The disappointments… violations… devastations of the years have piled high, unspoken upon my back. And now, I need catharsis. Yes, a good word for it, that …catharsis. And that is why…

I must let you touch my soul.

So, we will minister, soul to soul, deep to deep. That by journey's end, you will have befriended me. And, if I am fortunate, very fortunate, you will want to walk with me again.

You will have touched my soul.

So, here is the bargain that I shall offer you. I will tell you of the dreams that nightly wrench me from sleep. Shortly, we shall leave levity far behind. The currency of our conversation shall purchase richer fare. As we grow more familiar with each other, perhaps, I shall feel confident enough to declare my self-worth to you. As we walk from darkness into light, I shall come to trust you enough to tell you why I no longer need to keep my sword hand free.

Perhaps, you will allow me to introduce you to some friends of mine? The Biker is waiting to meet you. And if you are fortunate, very fortunate, I may also be able to effect an introduction to the Weaver – but I cannot promise. He is very shy, you know. And, will we touch the Tao that is the eternal Tao? Maybe … or any one of a thousand other thoughts that stir me to pain or passion and by which I know, I too, still live.

And your side of the bargain? … you know, already.

I want to touch your soul.

And when I have unleashed the demons and the angels that scream and cry for freedom… and when I am done touching your soul… you will tell me… please… because I really need to know…

Am I a writer?

2. Fly on a Windscreen

A fly lounged lazily on my windscreen
soaking up the Indian Summer sun.
Gossamer wings glistened,
as he stretched his legs,
ignorant in his complacency.
He did not know I watched him,
intrigued and faintly amused,
as I turned the engine over.
And as the car moved away,
he clung desperately to his comfortable spot
and struggled, flyfully,
'til the wind forced flight into his wings.
He soared.

A man lounged lazily in my body,
Watching youth's Indian Summer wane
Self satisfaction sparkled,
as he stretched his credibility,
ignorant in his complacency.
He did not know I watched him,
intrigued and faintly amused

as I turned his existence over.
And as his world moved away,
he clung desperately to his comfort zone
and struggled, manfully,
'til the Tao forced flight into his wings.
He's sore.

3. The Biker

I draw up to the traffic lights in the outside lane in order to turn right. I'm away in trance, thinking about nothing in particular, when I become aware of a motorcycle pulling up behind. He's woven his way through the traffic, but I've not left enough room between my car and the vehicle in the next lane to enable him to pass through. So, I sit, waiting for the lights to change, half listening to the throb coming from behind me. The silencer on the bike has been removed to turn up the volume. He revs the throttle impatiently, drawing an aggressive throaty growl from the engine that stands as the oratory of his impatience. His irritation is clearly growing. He is becoming angry at my having impeded his progress to the front of the traffic queue. Is he a Hell's Angel? Will he get off the bike and approach me? Will his anger boil over? Is road rage to follow? Will I be hauled unceremoniously from my car and thrown to the ground as he vents his frustration?

Then, I stop myself. I begin to reconsider all the value judgements we make as we pass, though, each day, our attention commonly focussed on ourselves. Will that woman be verbally aggressive to me? Is that man a threat to me? Is that child going to cross my path suddenly and trip me up?

Does this situation offer an opportunity for me to bolster my opinion of myself? Will that one diminish me in your eyes? Will this conflict harm me? How can I protect myself? How best can I make you esteem me?

We ride a veritable merry-go-round of self-focussed fear, revolving at the break-neck speed of unconscious thought, so ingrained in us, that we are largely unaware it is happening at all. Without realising what we are doing, we assess everything and everyone from the perspective of our own self interest, unless we have become aware of the pattern and unless our love has become unconditional. We throw up a force field of self-protective tension around ourselves that we allow no one to penetrate, unless we are sure, they are no threat. We isolate ourselves emotionally through fear. We touch in body but not in mind or heart. We seek to build ourselves up in the eyes of others, that we might seem more than we believe we really are, for we have learned to think of others as bigger, more attractive, more valuable than ourselves.

The images we hold of others have been larger than reality since childhood. The pain of young competition has taught us until we have fused the lesson into our neurology, that we must presume the universe to be a dangerous place, that other people must be assumed a danger to us until we have enough experience of them to know we are safe. So, we in turn learn to project an image of ourselves that is stronger, more capable, more articulate, more attractive, more admirable... more loveable than we really believe ourselves to be. Because we do not see ourselves as we are, as love has made us, we need to bolster our wizened images of our identity in the forlorn hope that others will perceive us to be more than we fear ourselves to be. For only then, can we believe they will think, we match up to the fantasy image of their innate superiority that we carry around inside ourselves. Only then, will we be safe. Only then will we be loveable. Only then, are we enough.

Of course, the problem is that everyone else is doing the same thing, as well. So, here we go, to and fro upon the earth, preoccupying our days with the projecting of vainglorious images that are intended to match the mirages we are receiving back; each of us, holding a magnifying glass to our identity, pretending to measure up to some unnecessary and unachievable standard we call superiority in a spiral of fictional frenzy that becomes ever more intense and ever less satisfying.

We choose the battlegrounds of identity enhancement to suit what we perceive to be our natural advantages – physical characteristics of beauty or strength, intellectual capabilities of the mind, strength of personality that yields power and control, gifts and talents – or the ubiquitous catch all of material possession. Never have the Jones' been more kept up with. Eventually, though, we arrive at the place where we have fought enough conflicts, reckoning our level relative to others with the unbalanced theodolites of perceived superiority. The battleground itself, then, comes to stand in our mind as representation of the identities we seek to bolster, and the trance is complete. I don't mind that I am less competent than you as (say) a deep sea diver or interior designer, for it holds no meaning for me. But challenge my perception of myself as (say) an outstanding apple picker, and I will react in anger. For I have come to hold apple picking as the centre of my universe. It is a metaphor for who I am. We can go through the whole of our lives like this, if we choose, living by the values of the child, perceiving ourselves as weak, unregarded or unlovable. And we can waste lifetime after lifetime, if we do not transcend the fears of the child we carry inside.

But if we are fortunate, eventually we come to see the strategy for what it is. It generally takes some epiphany of a life crisis before we recognise our self-manipulation. Then, it is that, at last we learn to take the energy we have applied to making ourselves feel safe, and instead, send it out to other hearts and souls around us, in an exploration driven by loving curiosity. We begin to touch the universe, as it is, for the first time in our lives and find it to be different from the self-protective trances in which we have slept so long. We learn that others are touchable, that they have hearts and souls, joys and pains, strengths and weaknesses and hopes and fears, just as we do. And when we touch another who responds with aggression, it no longer forces us back into a protective shell, our former view of the universe reconfirmed for a negative eternity. For we realise that here is a soul who has simply, yet, to learn the way the universe is, to realise that the body is made of energy and the soul was made to love unconditionally. Then, it is that all those fatuous crutches – emotional, intellectual, physical or material – that we used to need, now, seem somehow unimportant. We bury them at sea, without sadness or remorse. We watch them slowly slip away from under the ensign of our identity.

I do not need to impress you any more. I do not need to fear you any more. For your heart is as my heart is. Your soul is here on a life contract, just as mine is. You are my brother, my sister, my mother, my father. Loving you is as natural as loving myself. The fog of the trance is burned away in the unremitting midday sunlight of higher truth revealed. The battlegrounds matter no longer, for we ourselves no longer feel the need to be bigger than the other person. We are content to be as we are. And in so being, we have started upon the road to self-realisation and growth of the soul. We have, perhaps, at last begun the learning that we need to imbibe for this lifetime.

So, let's go back to that biker revving his engine behind me in the traffic queue. Has he cloaked himself with images of power, or have I wound him in the swaddling clothes of my own unresolved childhood fear? Who creates the barrier between the biker and me? Is it his unconscious acts of self-enhancement or my nightmare monsters, loosed from the bowels of my dream world? Or, is it perhaps, no more than a car window and twenty feet of empty air?

The lights change and the motorcyclist slips through the gap that was always there, between the car in the next lane and mine. He roars away to his day's work as a nursery school teacher, a spiritual healer or a civil servant sitting in a drab grey office.

I make my right turn, catch a familiar face and wave as I pass. The trance is over. I have reached beyond my self-protective shell and touched another's reality. In this lifetime, he will never know he has edified me.

4. From the Darkness

I looked for love.
I thought she hid her huddled heart
in corners dark
defiled by rank cold smells
where cobwebs covered dust strewn floors of lonely sentiment.

I called her name.
Too sad was she, I thought, to answer me,
for memories of pleasures past
and fear of future's numb futility.

To my surprise
she came to me;
discovered me;
threw open wide the windows of my soul
'til sunlight streamed upon my tear-stained face
and I discovered in my shock
that it was I, not her,
that dwelt in deep forgotten dungeons
of my soul.

No judge passed sentence on my lonely heart.
No man decreed that chained in isolation I should dwell.
The choice was only mine to live,
incarceration self imposed in hellish night
and desperation's solitary cell.

Love smiled at me,
and took my hand.
She led me from the dungeons
wherein I chained my weary, saddened soul;
in gentle urgings drew me to the light
and bade me step in confidence
beyond the grasping clutch
of introspective demons that held sway.

I held her close
and launched with her to lands as yet unknown.
I knew inside the fear I fled
was left behind in darkness
when finally, I yielded to the light.

5. Declaration of Self Worth

Weep and heal, my friend, weep and heal. And, as you weep, anoint me with the tears that wash away your pain, that I, too, may take the healing you pour into your weeping.

We have allowed the leaches to bleed us dry, for fear of losing what we never had.

We have listened until mesmerised by the words that proclaim our inadequacies in the eyes of another. We have screamed in silent agony at the withdrawal of conditional love whose requirements we can no longer satisfy. We have shaken in misery at the prospect of losing love that was not love.

We have been fashioned in the same furnace, you and I. We have held the same pain in our hearts, giving until we can give no more. We have faced the same dark pit of depression and learned slowly and painfully to drag ourselves up its rocky walls. We have emerged from the edge with bleeding hands and knees, but stronger, much stronger in the knowledge that we are survivors.

We have recognised that without unconditional love, there is no life worth clinging to. We have contemplated death in the face of loneliness. We have reached beyond the limits of endurance and known the angels stoop to carry us when we can walk no more. We have sat in silent meditation and confronted lives of transparent emptiness for future decades that we believe we cannot endure.

We have acknowledged our own fault-line cracks, confronted our own weaknesses and declared them to be intrinsic to our humanity. We have asserted our need, our right to be loved for who we are, not for what we give or for how effectively we transform ourselves into that, which the object of our love would have us be.

We are resolute: no more will we cut our hands and feet as we dance around the altar of another's whims in forlorn hope that our Deity will come to ignite the sacrifice. No more will we throw the children of our own undeveloped aspirations into the volcanoes of appeasement to placate the angry gods and goddesses.

We have taken the surgeon's knife of separation to the cancer of co-dependency in a final act of self-absolution.

We will no longer supplicate with the congregations of the acquiescent that worship in the cathedrals of self-deprecation.

We have determined, that NOW, is the time to rise, that NOW, we shall reach for the light, that NOW, we shall claim our birth right in the grace of new intimacy, that NOW, we shall lay hold of the promise of infusing joy.

We are the survivors of love grown cold.

We have learned that we are worthy.

6. Flash in the Pan

An ethereal vicissitude ferments anticipation;
strews molting tufts of coalescing consciousness
across the beckoning portals of yestermorrow.

She has morning eyes,
This Grace;
This Essence;
This Familiar,

crystalising awareness
from the cooling mud pools
of primeval monotony;

chipping at the jagged corners
with flint chisels of mortality;

patiently panning the silt
of past life patterns.

Elevated to this windswept crag,
I can see clear across the valley of this incarnation
and on into the next.

7. The Negotiators

He reminded me of me, in a way, right from that first telephone, call, asking if it was I, who had placed the "for sale" advertisement in the paper. I was to leave my home shortly, and was selling off the accoutrements of middle-class country living – a lawn tractor, garden tools, ladders and so on. These I had assembled over the preceding three or four years, all necessary items in the management of a country house, yet, now, superfluous to the path I was shortly to tread.

Possessions had come to mean less and less to me over that time. I know it's easy to be blasé about material goods when you have plenty; much harder to live without wealth when you are hungry, or cold, or can't buy a toy to coax a smile from the eyes of a crying child. I do not mean to devalue material objects, or their rightful place in our lives. It is simply, I have noted that the appeal of "things" consistently diminishes with their acquisition. There is a hunger associated with materialism that evidences itself, only during the period before we acquire the object of our desire. Its intensity varies, depending on the importance the item has in the representation we make of it, and the degree of satisfaction we believe it will bring to us. Very often, it arises because we anticipate the possession of such an item makes an identity statement about us: I'm the kind of person who drives... I'm the kind of person who wears... I'm the kind of person who owns... and so on. In extreme cases, that hunger becomes so all-pervasive that we are unable to function properly, so great is the interference of that representation. Eventually, we do what we need to do to possess the object of our desire. In some cases the consequences are devastating, to both ourselves and the people around us. It is most likely to be so when that which we seek to possess is not an object, but rather another person.

Commonly, possession of the item reframes its value in our mind to such an extent that we find ourselves wondering why we had desired it so intensely in the first place. Rarely, have I ever found something I wanted to be as satisfying in its possession, as I had represented it to be in its anticipation. If we are fortunate, we learn after a while that material items are incapable of satisfying an eternal soul. We learn the lesson and come to focus our attentions on matters of edification and the learning of the pathway we have come here to tread. If we are less fortunate, we fail to learn that lesson, running and re-running the pattern with item after item, circumstance after circumstance and perhaps, even person after person. If you observe someone in such a state you can almost hear the heart cry, almost see the hunger in the form of a tangible entity, as they focus determinedly on the next object of desire, only to feel the elusive satisfaction slip away with its acquisition. They are left with only the insatiate hunger ever remaining, drawing them to the next item and the next, in a never ending chain of unfulfillable hopes. This is the tragedy of a material dominated life style.

But what of my negotiator? As it happened, he was the first to respond to my advertisement, showing interest in a dovecote I had advertised for sale. We had bought the house with the dovecote already in place in the garden. I had removed it from its spot some three years previously, because we were undertaking ground works that first summer we had arrived in the house. So little value had I attached to it, that I had placed it in an empty stable, and more or less forgotten about it since that time. Now, I was leaving, and it was time to sell it on. Knowing that these objects were currently retailing new for around £500.00, I advertised it at £150.00, eventually receiving five enquiries in all.

My negotiator friend sounded excited when I told him, his was the first call I had received in response to my ad. He wanted to visit immediately. If I had paid more attention to his tone during that conversation, I might have sensed more readily that he had the air of the hunter about him, as one who has heard the jungle drums and smelled the blood of the prey, as he closed in for the kill. Thirty minutes later, he appeared on my doorstep. He wanted to negotiate from the moment he arrived, his eyes roving over the house and garden in search of anything he might deem to be of value and be able to acquire for less than his perception of its worth. I'm a well-trained negotiator myself, and I know the routines of trading thoroughly. I suppressed a wry smile as I saw so many of my own former strategies and tactics reflected in my visitor's manner. Generally speaking, I have lost the urge to win a few extra inches of ground in a negotiation now. There are other concerns that preoccupy me more. However, it's always interesting to look back on our former selves reflected in the ways of another.

He took one look at my dovecote and was smitten. Given the cost of a new equivalent and the state of the object, the price I asked seemed very reasonable to me. But there was a principle at stake here; one that went far beyond the item that was the subject of our discussion. For no matter how valuable it was to him, it now had to be accorded a status of tainted unpleasantness, something to be criticised and inherently devalued. For in so doing, he would diminish its worth in my eyes and achieve a better price. He would perceive himself to win and me to lose. And in so doing he would diminish my worth and achieve an enhanced view of himself in both our eyes.

He prodded at the dovecote, commenting on the absence of various features and the amount of work he would have to undertake in order to bring the offending item to an acceptable state. He put his hands in his pockets and circled it slowly, sniffing disinterestedly from time to time. There was no doubt at all that he was going to buy it. The only question was how far he could beat me down on the price; how easily he could draw me into his map of the world, so as to see that I had grossly overvalued the item and how much of a favour he was doing me by removing it from my garden; how my life would actually be enhanced, were he, to take this problem away from me, there and then.

And what of my own part in all of this? Well, I have to admit that sometimes, old habits have a tendency to rise like vampires from their shallow buried coffins just when you least want them to. I'd like to tell you, that, that day, I was more concerned with the state of my visitor's heart than the contents of his wallet. I'd like to be able to say that I saw through my own tendencies and patterns, clearly enough to resist the pull of the past; that I could see the incompatibility of unconditional love that puts soul states first, with a strategy that treats them as ego fodder and thus, puts them last. But unfortunately, I didn't. My former way of being rose again, and my dovecote became an object of exquisite desire, a family heirloom, the loss of which would cause separation anxiety to my children and my children's children for decades to come. My ability to win the negotiation over that dovecote which I had ignored for the last three years was as much a statement of my self worth, as it was his.

Finally, he offered two thirds of the asking price. I recoiled in shock, distraught at his offensive assessment of its near inestimable value. I breathed smelling salts to revive myself from shock. I tore my clothes and sat in ashes. I looked fondly at my beloved possession.. I dropped my price ten pounds.

I won't bore you with the details. Eventually, our horse trading arrived at a compromise solution and he went on his way, no doubt, planning to tell the story at that evening's dinner party of the bargain he had hunted down that morning. I don't begrudge him the pleasure he will take in either the dovecote or his recounting of his own negotiating skills. But, after he had gone, I did get to thinking about what we had done; how we had each come near to selling our souls that day, or at the very least, placing a monetary value on self-esteem. I believe we were both diminished by that process. For each of us could have chosen to give way, he, to buy at the asking price or I, to accept what was offered. Neither of us would have noticed the monetary difference. Neither of us could do so, though, for what was at stake was not a dovecote or a few pounds in cash, but our views of our own self-worth. Each of us relied on our ability to out-negotiate the other, in order to esteem ourselves as valuable.

Is his soul really worth to me only the twenty-five pounds I coaxed out of him over and above his offer price that day? I don't think so. I haven't even banked the cash yet.

8. Flying Fish

And we are but flying fish
breaking the surface for a moment
to bask in the reflected glory
of a transient elevation.

9. Reflections

The major elements that once I would have regarded as defining the parameters of my life have now largely passed, registering but minor tremors on the seismograph of my identity. The consequential features of what job I did, where I lived, what I owned, faded away long ago almost unnoticed. It is emotion that has formed me; the pain of rejection; the elation of love; the depression of marginalisation, and the silent screams of abandonment. These are the Richter-registering events that have raised up my valleys and laid low my mountains. For our humanity is defined not by cars and houses, lotteries and vacations. We are who we are because of the ghosts of the past that still walk beside us. The ethereal spectres of unfulfillment that haunt our dreams and aspirations are the intimate companions of our souls; these, together with the karmas of the contemporaries we brush against, as we pass blindly through the darkened forests of present experience and as we walk daily, unknowingly, over our own graves.

You build a life without realising you're doing it. One moment you're living in an unheated room with holes in the elbows of your sweater. The next, you turn around and the badges of opulence are draped casually around your

Olympian self-satisfaction. You look at the semi, the executive car, the wife and the 2.4 and you sigh in relief at the crystal wall you have erected to hide your insecurity. You've chosen flawed crystal, of course, attracted by its opaqueness in the vain hope that no one will see through to the serpent's nest inside. You fool nobody but yourself.

Then, some inconceivable intrusion of reality take a hammer to the crystal. It shatters, exposing the seething mass of terrors undefined that always did writhe silently, just below the shining shell. The material universe on which you had come to rely is gone, a pile of dreams lying at your feet. At first, you pick at the pieces in your incomprehension, for the destruction of the crystal shell is inconceivable to you. You must rebuild it from what is left. Then, having lacerated your palms and your soles in a frantic bid at restoration, you kneel, quiescent in horror-struck denial, amongst the shining shards.

Eventually, the abject terror you felt at the consequences of your loss begins to abate. Denial turns to depression and then, gradually to anger, to acceptance, in accordance with the well-worn steps of this bizarre ballet we call recovery. And gradually, imperceptibly, you come to see it: everything you ever employed to buttress your insecurity was only, a product of the resources you possess inside yourself; that you were the person who attracted those energies into your life; that it was you who took those leaden circumstances and alchemised them into the gold you held in such awe; that all of your achievements, all of that, which you valued, first started as no more than primeval, conceptual thought, gliding upon the troposphere of your soul.

And then, you realise that you could do it all over again if you wanted to; if you needed to. But somehow, it isn't important any more. Once you understand that you have already sucked the marrow of experience from the bones of that particular gestalt, you realise that it is irrefutably time to move on; for these are the hammers and the chisels that the spirits use to sculpt enlightenment into our stony souls.

In moving on, it is only the people I will miss from that other existence, now, filed in padlocked mental cabinets marked "top secret – open only when seated before roaring log fires of reminiscence." Some of them still remain within the new paradigm, of course. But they are not as they were. They are not who they were. For they have gone on to fashion themselves with tools I have neither seen nor understood. They model their ways of being with new values and new expectations, in which I cannot, do not, share as once I did. These are they, whom once I knew; with whom I danced to the waltzes of long-forgotten orchestras, the soul-touch bringing inexpressible joy and screaming frustrations down upon us in equal measure – the experiences that make a life more than a mere existence. Those relationships are gone now; laid into neat rows, hands upon their chests, with headstones erected in silent testimony to our inherent transience. Mortality is made of commencements and completions.

The only possession we carry with us beyond the grave is our learning. The only substance in the universe we cannot replicate is spirit.

10. Seeking Space

Seek me not in the words
but in the spaces in between;
not in the come go turn-a-day of turning days
but clothed in the cloistered twilight
that shrouds ephemeral voids of softening silence.

Not in the plainsong chiming hour
will you find the nest of plenitude,
nor where gnostic whips unfurl
to curl across the cursed coerced,
inscribed upon Abraxas stones.

I am not found on carousels of power where
Parliaments of rooks and crooks
adjudicate the codicils of Piety,
nor yet within the bustling market places of the garrulous.

Seek me in that somnolent space
-you know it well –
where shimmering shadows meet to
treat and trick the eye

and try the slowing heart to reach for trailing
vines that tremble in the undertow.

You will find me
sat at the feet of journeys un-commenced
where solitude apprentices her trade
and touchstones mumble half forgiven heresies;
where warriors wield ploughshares
and angels watch while learned
men dance solemnly upon the heads of pins.

Unknowing here shall compensate
the quenchant fires of absolution and
new birthed immortality unfurled
shall bid the Uninitiate come enter in
this place where endings find beginnings.

11. The Weaver

Chapter I

1. In the beginning, God created the heavens and the earth. And upon the sixth day, made he man. Whereupon, the Lord God did rest from his labours and saw that they were good.

2. And when the Lord did rest, so did the works of man prosper. And each took his chosen course and did labour with joy, the praises of the Lord to sing with his industry.

3. And in that day, did the Weaver labour at his loom. And the Lord did look upon the Weaver and did smile, for diligently, the man attended to his given task.

4. But the Lord, God, was concerned that so diligent was the Weaver, that he might forget the purpose whereunto He had placed him upon the earth.

5. So, the Lord called unto the Weaver and spoke to him in the night as he lay upon his bed saying, "My son, dost thou remember, why I had made the heavens and the earth?"

6. "Yea, Lord," answered the Weaver. "Thou hast set the stars in their courses that they might sing thy praises. Thou hast set the cycles of the season that they might speak of thy glory. Thou hast set man upon the earth that he might know Thee.

And thou set the Weaver at the loom that he might learn and know his own soul."

7. "Well hast thou spoken, my son," said the Lord unto the Weaver. But have thou care that when thou dost labour diligently, thou dost not forget to look upon thine own soul.

8. And lest, thou should forget, I have imparted a gift unto thee." And when He had, thus, spoken, the Lord departed from the Weaver.

9. The morning light did come and the Weaver did awake to find the gift of the Lord at his right hand.

10. And when the Weaver reached out his hand to touch the Lord's gift, he held within his grasp a mirror, framed in wood, its glass polished as the sun.

11. Then, did he gaze into the mirror and his soul did he see, therein. And the Weaver did love the gift of the Lord. Thus, as he worked at his loom and did his tapestries make, oft would he gaze into the mirror and see his soul.

12. And as oft as he would do this, was he reminded of his purpose ordained by the Lord – to know his soul and therein, his God to worship.

13. And it came to pass in those days that the Weaver was cumbered about with much weaving. And of the making of tapestries was there no end. For greatly did men revere the handiwork of the Weaver, and princes and kings would vie for the fruit of the Weaver's loom.

14. And the Weaver did look upon his work and knew that it was good and knew that his industry supported his family, and bread unto the mouths of his children did it bring.

15. But as much as the Weaver did labour, so did his needs grow yet more. Thus, did it seem to him, that his industry would never meet his needs. And moreover, more than a little joy did the Weaver take in the love of kings for the labour of his hands.

16. And it came to pass that the labour of the day made weariness in the heart of the Weaver. Then, it was that he did stop and looked not into the mirror that the Lord, his God, had given unto him.

17. Always would the Weaver, his mirror carry. Always would it be at his side. Yet, took he not the time to look into the mirror, his own soul to know.

Chapter II

1. It came to pass one spring that the Weaver was summoned by a certain king in a far off land, to attend upon him with his tapestries at his palace.

2. Then, the Weaver hitched his oxen and did pile high upon his cart, the fruit of his loom and of his labour. And when he looked upon the work of his hands, then, did he know that it was good. And upon the pile of tapestries, did the Weaver his mirror lay and did bid the oxen draw the cart.

3. And it came to pass in those days that as the Weaver made his way unto the palace, he needs must cross a certain fast flowing river.

4. As the oxen entered the ford of the river, so as to cross, then, did one of their number stumble. And the tapestries did make as if to fall from the cart. Then, sore afraid was the Weaver that the works of his hands would be destroyed.

5. Thus, it was that he sought as if to hold the tapestries upon the cart. And as he did so, then did the mirror slip from the cart and fall into the river. And the glass of the mirror did shatter and the shards of glass were carried away into the fast flowing water.

6. But the frame of the mirror did lodge fast, caught in the reeds.

7. Then, the Weaver looked upon the frame of the mirror and the shards, as they were carried far from him. Then, did he understand what he had done. And his hands rose from the tapestries and the tapestries did fall into the water and they, too, were carried from his view.

8. The Weaver reached into the reeds where the frame of the mirror was lodged and he did take the frame of the mirror, and look upon it. But the Weaver did not see his soul, for the glass of the mirror was gone.

9. Then, did the Weaver, his oxen lead, and they drew the empty cart unto to his home.

10. And the Weaver lay upon his bed and turned his face unto the wall. And he would not be comforted.

11. Then, did he fall into a deep sleep. And in the sleep the Weaver dreamed a dream. And in that dream, he came unto the Lord, his God, holding in his hand the frame of the mirror.

12. And the Lord said to the Weaver, "Hast thou considered thy soul, my son? Hast thou looked upon it in the mirror that I have given thee?"

13. Then, was the Weaver ashamed. "Nay, Lord," answered he, "I did not look into my mirror and for so long, I did not see my soul that I forgot who I am and why thou didst put me upon the earth. And now, the mirror is broken and the glass is gone and I cannot remember the appearance of my soul."

14. "What dost thou, now, desire of me? " said the Lord unto the Weaver. And the Weaver answered and said unto his God, "Lord, wilt thou give me another mirror that I might contemplate my soul and be reminded why thou has placed me upon the earth?"

15. Then, was the Lord silent and spake not.

16. So again, the Weaver did lift up his voice and spoke thus,

to the Lord, his God, saying, "By Thy silence, Lord, is my foolishness revealed unto me. For there is only one mirror to the soul and therein, must I look if I am to see who it is, that I am and why it is that thou hast placed me upon the earth."

17. "Rightly, hast thou spoken my son," said the Lord unto the Weaver. "Go in peace. Grow in grace."

18. And the Weaver, then, did know the task where unto he would set himself. And he did know that it was the work of his life to find the shards of his mirror and therein, to contemplate his soul.

19. So, the Weaver gathered up all that which he did need and made to leave behind the many that he had known and had loved. And they did not wish him Godspeed but did bid him stay, saying, "Take thine ease. Many goods are lain up to thine old age and merry shall be thy part. What matters it, if thou canst not see thy soul. Time is enough for thee to find a new mirror. Come, eat, drink, be merry, for tomorrow is thine."

20. But the Weaver, having set his eyes unto the road, would not be distracted from his quest. For though comfort and rest called unto him, he knew his soul, called, yet louder, to be seen and to be known.

Chapter III

1. And as the Weaver did journey in the way, there, did he come upon a Mason. And the Mason called unto the Weaver saying, "Hail traveller!" Canst thou spare a day, for I labour upon the building of a temple and all my workers have forsaken me."

2. And the Weaver thought to say unto the Mason, "Nay, for I seek the shards of my mirror with which to see the facets of my soul." But moved was he to tarry and to help the Mason

as he did build his edifice, that it might be a glory unto the Lord.

3. And the Mason and the Weaver laboured all that day together. And they did come to know each other. Thus, did the Weaver touch the soul of the Mason, the temple builder, and both their hearts were soothed. Then, when the evening came, together they took their rest.

4. And the evening and the morning were the first day.

Chapter IV

1. When the morning light broke, then, did the Mason speak unto the Weaver and say, "Stay with me, my friend, and together we will build edifices unto the Lord. But the Weaver answered and said unto him, "Nay, I am but a Weaver and the shards of my mirror, I must find, that I might contemplate my soul.

2. Then, did he take his leave and did continue upon his journey.

3. And as he did proceed upon his way, the sun rose high in its course. Thus, it was that when he came upon a well, he did break his journey there. Then, the Weaver drew water from the well with which to quench his thirst. And as he drank, unto the well, a beggar came, lame and blind.

4. When the Blind Beggar did perceive he was not alone at the well, he called out, "Friend, wilt thou draw water for me, for I cannot see where to place my hands for to drink."

5. And though, his heart was set upon the continuance of his journey, the Weaver did take the hands of the Beggar and did place them upon the well rope. Thus, could the beggar draw water for himself and quench his thirst.

6. And when the Beggar had drunk his fill, he turned and

spake unto the Weaver saying, "Friend, oft times did I come to the well and many have drawn water for me. But none did place my hands upon the well rope that I might learn to draw for myself. And now, I am taught how to draw water, never again, shall I thirst or need a man to draw for me. But I shall come to the well as I choose and shall drink my fill."

7. Then, the Blind Beggar lifted up his hands and did bless the Weaver. And the Weaver placed his arms about the beggar and held him to his heart in gratitude for his blessing. And the Weaver knew that he had touched the soul of the beggar.

8 And the Weaver did proceed upon his way and did journey until the night did fall. And he took his rest under a tree.

9 And the evening and the morning were the second day.

Chapter V

1. Thus it was, when the sun did rise that the Weaver was hungry. For two days had he travelled without sustenance. So, he rose from that place and unto a town did come. And there would he seek work, that he might buy food before proceeding upon his way.

2. And as he made to enter the gates of the town, sitting in the gates did he see the Elders. And discourse did they make amongst themselves.

3. So, the Weaver tarried in that place and listened to the Elders as they did speak. And one of the Elders turned to the Weaver and said unto him, "Welcome, sojourner. Art thou a man of learning? For we have a message from God that is written in a language that no man here can read. Is this thy native tongue and canst thou perchance tell us the meaning of the message?"

4. Then, did the Weaver look upon the paper that the Elder

did offer him, and saw that nothing was written thereon. And the Weaver did perceive the meaning of the wordless message that God had sent unto the elders of the town.

5. And the Weaver lifted up his voice and spoke unto the Elders, saying, "Yea, this is in a language that I have learned with much aching of the heart and searching of the soul to speak. The Lord, thy God, would say unto thee that his laws shall be written upon thy hearts and upon thy hands, and not in books. Then, thou shalt think the thoughts and work, the works of thy God."

6. And the Elders of the town knew that the Weaver spoke the truth.

7. Then, the Elders lifted up their voices as one and gave glory unto God. And they did beseech the Weaver to tarry with them and to teach them. But he would not, saying, "When the laws of thy God are written upon thy hearts and upon thy hands, then, thou shalt read words of God and know their meaning. "And the Weaver knew that he had touched the souls of the elders of the town.

8. Then, the Weaver departed and continued upon his course. Far did he travel, but still he did not find the shards he sought.

9. And the evening and the morning were the third day.

Chapter VI

1. Then, it was that the Weaver continued in his way. And three days had he travelled and still no sign had he seen of the shards of his mirror. Then was his heart heavy within him, for he thought that never again would he see his soul.

2. And it came to pass that a Warrior from a foreign land did stand within the way and said unto the Weaver, "Hold, enemy! Take up thy sword and do battle with me here and

now. For I am champion of my land and would subjugate thy people.

3. And the Weaver did look upon the Warrior and was filled with compassion for one that knew only how to take hold of a sword for war, and not how to take hold of a hand for love.

4. Then, did the Weaver draw his sword, but only to place it at the feet of the Warrior. And he did look into the warrior's eyes and did see such anger and pain as cannot be told.

5. And the Weaver took the Warrior into his arms and did kiss him upon the cheek and did say unto him, "I call thee brother – take thy peace."

6. And the Warrior dropped his sword and did weep the tears of pain that he had ever carried in his war making. For the Weaver had touched his soul.

7. And the evening and the morning were the fourth day.

Chapter VII

1. The Weaver rose up early upon the next morn. And yet again, did he commence the search for the shards of his mirror. For he was no nearer to finding them and could not look upon his soul. Thus, deeply was he troubled that the task whereunto he had set himself he could not fulfill.

2. As he journeyed abroad, he came upon a Traveller who had been set upon by thieves. And the man did lie bleeding at the roadside, for he had been grievously treated and was in great pain.

3. Then, the Weaver took water from a brook and first did he revive the Traveller by moistening his lips. Then did he wash his wounds and rent asunder his own raiment to make bandages to bind the wounds of the traveller.

4. And he took the Traveller to a place of safety, then made

as if to leave. The traveller spake unto him saying, "Stay, let me repay thee, for thou hast healed my body and thereby, touched my soul.

5. But the Weaver did know full well his task was to journey until he did find the shards of his mirror and therein to see his soul. For only thus, could he know his purpose upon the earth.

6. And the evening and the morning were the fifth day.

Chapter VIII

1. Thus, it came to pass, that the Weaver did despair of ever finding the shards. And he sat beside the road and wept for the loss of his soul.

2. And as he wept, did a Philosopher sit beside him and spoke unto him saying, "Why dost thou weep?

3. And the Weaver lifted up his voice and said unto the Philosopher, "I have lost my mirror and I cannot see my soul."

4. And the Philosopher answered and said unto him, "There is no need to see thy soul. Look upon the works of man both of mind and of hand and see what he has done."

5. Then, deep into the night the Philosopher and the Weaver held discourse. And the Weaver did cleave fast to the truth, but nothing could the philosopher sway.

6. Then, did the morning light come and the Philosopher rose to leave. For he would not let the Weaver touch his soul.

7. And the evening and the morning were the sixth day.

Chapter IX

1. Then, in his exhaustion, fell the Weaver into a deep sleep. And in the sleep did he dream another dream.

2. And in his dream did the Lord God come unto him and said unto the Weaver "My son, in all thy travelling, didst thou find the shards of thy mirror?

3. And the Weaver answered and said unto Him, "Lord, in six days didst thou make the heavens and the earth, man, and the Weaver. And for six days I have travelled and searched for the shards of my mirror but have found them not. My soul is weary unto death. Take me home."

4. And the Lord answered and said unto him, "Tell me whom thou didst meet as thou didst journey in the way."

5. And the Weaver answered, "I met a Mason whom I helped." And the Lord said unto the Weaver "Dost thou not see that I have made thee a Builder? Teach men to create edifices of the spirit for my glory. Whom else didst thou meet?"

6. And Weaver answered, "A Beggar, Lord, to whom I brought water."

7. "My son," said the Lord "hast thou not seen that I have made thee a Diviner? Thou shalt show men how to draw water from the wells of their own souls. Whom else didst thou meet?"

8. "An Elder Lord," replied the Weaver, "for whom I interpreted thy teachings."

9. "My son," said the Lord, "dost thou not see that I have made thee a Teacher. Speak wisdom to the wise that have ears to hear my truth. Whom else didst thou meet?"

10. "A Warrior, Lord, who did bid me do battle with him. But I kissed him for the sake of thy love."

11. "Thou art a Priest my son," said the Lord. "Ever thou must lay down thy sword on the altar of war for the sake of my love and my truth. Whom else didst thou meet?

12. "A Traveller, Lord," answered the Weaver, "who had been set upon by thieves. To him did I offer the simple friendship of humanity."

13 "Thou art a Physician my son," said the Lord. "Thy words must be balm that drip with healing from thy spirit that is within thee, restoring the souls of men. And whom finally didst thou meet?"

14. "I met a Philosopher, Lord, whose soul I could not touch and who would not hear thy words."

15. "Then, know this, my son, thou art a Guardian. Be steadfast in the truth of love when the mind of man doth overreached itself.

16. My son," said the Lord unto the Weaver, "in all thy travelling, didst thou find what thou didst seek?"

17. "Yea Lord," said the Weaver, "I have found my soul. "

12. Anteroom

Words, superfluous here,
forsake the come-go bustle
of ostentatious decibels,
to bow their lofty resonance
before the feet of silence.

Falling free;
the fear unfurls
where trust weaves calm
in gentle hems of heart-held expectation.

Treading soft as silence
on velvet meadows of serenity;
passing through the anterooms of peace;
enter the portals of the Innermost
where love sits.

And waits.

13. Lessons from the death of a marriage

The awareness has flowed in deep channels this year, long and deep, stretching as far as the eye can see back into the history of my predestination fulfilled. I have learned of my origins, the patterns of my childhood, set as much in the karma of other souls as in my own. I have learned how we came together now, the purpose of our union, the learning that has come which could be mine by no other means.

We were soul mates, she and I. The cords that linked us one to the other were strong, entwined so tightly as to be all but indistinguishable. For years, each of us lived our union in fear that the other might die, that we might lose a love so strong that fed our hearts and our bodies and our spirits. But I had not understood the way of souls so clearly at that time. I had thought we walked the earth for but one lifetime; that it was appointed unto man to live and die but once, and then, the one and final judgement. Had I realised sooner the ways of spirit, I might not have permitted her to hold me so tightly, or clung onto her myself in the way I did.

It seemed to me then, that she was a younger soul than I; that she drank deeply from me, and at that time, I had not learned to draw from the wells of eternity. The years took their toll. I seemed to exhaust myself in slaking her thirst until I, too, was parched and desperate for water. It was then, that love began to falter, tainted by resentment. "What is there for me?" I cried, for my own thirst was unabated. And, at the mention of the word 'me', the love began to decay, withering on the branch in the cool autumn mornings of self-centredness.

We did not see it at first. It came as to a tree in canker. The discolouration of our love took time to become visible, for the branches to lose their sap and harden into the brittleness of impending death. Those around us then and now, tell us that our union wore that autumnal look for years, yellowed by the jaundice of interest self-served. We ourselves were the last to see it, for neither of us would acknowledge the impending death of love. So tightly had the cords been wound, that to cease to love, to cease to be together, was inconceivable to either of us.

Had we been wiser, older souls, we might have seen the signs; might have realised that to be a soul mate is not always a state that lasts a life time, but rather, is one in need of constant nurturing by the mutual preference of another above the interests of the self. It might have come more easily to us if we had loved and left; if we had cut the cords cleanly in respect and friendship. But for us, it could not be so. The life we shared expired of slow strangulation, each of us heaving upon those cords that joined us; each of us seeking to draw the other more closely into line with our perceptions of reality and the future, we each believed, we needed.

It is hard beyond expression to lose one you love to physical death. It is, to my mind, much harder, yet, to watch and participate in the quietus of love itself.

My spirit guides have shown me much since then; a great deal of it by dawning realisation rather than direct infusion of knowledge into the mind. That is more commonly their way with me. The lightening bolts are few, the coming of the sun in golden dawns more frequent. That understanding is a salve to my heart, making it easier to live beyond the termination of the relationship in which I was indeed joined soul to soul. I know now, that to be so joined may indeed, last a lifetime, and on occasions, lifetimes. But this is not always necessarily so.

I have learned that she was not, as I once told her, half my soul and I half hers. I have learned that I am a person, an expression of the Divine in my own right. I have learned that I am valid, able to live as an individual, in touch with heaven on my own account, feet upon the earth for the purposes of my own learning and growth.

I have slipped her gentle touch now. She will walk her path as I walk mine; different paths, neither better nor worse, hers the way of the therapist, mine of poetry in the soul. She will have her lessons to learn, just as I will seek to open myself to the new possibilities pertaining to my karma from here forward. There may yet be another soul mate for me in this lifetime. If so, I will be joined once again for edification, for benefit, for truth and for love. And when my time comes to pass once more from this body, as I have done so many, many times before, she and I will come to acknowledge each other in the clarity of full awareness. We will make our reconciliation, as we understand the roles we each fulfilled in the life of the other. As the Christian once put it, "For now, I see, as through a glass, darkly, but then, face to face." There is much that we need to learn in the clouded reflection of the dim glass where we see ourselves imperfectly. Its tarnished opaqueness serves our edification well. But ultimately, there is reconciliation and acknowledgment of deeper truths when we see face to face.

This knowledge is my bedrock for the future. Within its solid, unyielding reassurance, I shall sink my new foundations. Upon it, I shall build my walls of security and portals of peace. These are the learnings that I have learned. Thus far, this has been the karma of my soul.

14. Guardians

And here I shall sleep safely
bounded by my unseen brethren,
whose silent roars protect,
vaulting the pitch
of fleshbound ears,
custodians of my purposes and paths,
saviours from my own uncertainty,
guardians of knowledge beyond my doubt
of who and what and why I am.

15. Making Her Peace

It was around two months ago that I entered upon a process of spiritual healing. I was, and still am, inexperienced in the ways of spirit touch. But so far had my internal state deteriorated, so close was I to drowning amongst the towering waves, that I was ready to reach out for any life belt that came to hand. And so, it was, I found myself with the Healer. She spoke of chakras and crystals, spirit guides and teachers, energy and auras. I had no resources inside with which to believe or disbelieve. I needed whatever help she could offer me. Though, I was sceptical, my confidence in her was greatly enhanced by the fact that she made no formal charge for the work she did, leaving each client to pay her in whatever way and to whatever level they were able. I trust people easily if they prove to be non-manipulative.

That first day, she sat me upon an upright chair in the middle of her lounge, placed a crystal in my left hand and told me to visualise turning on taps at the ends of my fingers and toes. The water I saw gushing out was near to black, silted with the darkness of the disempowering pain that was held in stasis within the neurology of my body. It was to be some weeks of healing sessions before that water began to run clean. The Healer stood over me as I dropped willingly into trance, her only concern, to clear my heart and aura and chakras from the accumulated dross of the pain that laced my history. She was workman like, willing to get right down into the muck, motioning and gesturing as if physically clearing the dirt from me with her hands. The session ended when she was satisfied she had done enough, and she brought me back into full consciousness before sending me on my way.

I left her house that day with no particular immediate benefit. It was perhaps three days later that the changes began. The snake of depression had long since wound itself around my heart, crushing even the recollections of joy in the misery of loss and memories of guilt. It began to lift; not comprehensively at first, but just a little, such that the burden of the pain was not beyond my ability to bear it. As the weeks proceeded, each session took me further out into the high country of possible futures, and I began to draw away from the jungle of overbearing darkness that had haunted my potential so long.

Often, I would look back, only to be overwhelmed with a sense of the amputation of my past, a life now lost but still sensed by its absence. History lived on in my heart then, as indeed it does now. But at that time, I had not learned to reconcile the passion and the pain, the joy and the frustration that make up the learning process of human growth, the life that we pre-plan for ourselves and come here to experience. I have come to understand a little better now, how to honour my past, how to live with the apparent incongruence of extremes of capability that are intrinsic to our nature; how to acknowledge my capacity for depth as well as height, darkness as much as light, without giving in to unrestrained self deprecation. I have learned something of the nature of humanity by gazing into my own soul. I do not store these recollections in the mausoleums of my memory gloating, miser-like, over a treasure-trove of personal history. Rather, I encourage my past to lie as foundation to my present and my future. I permit the shale and the limestone of each experience, integrated into unconscious learning, to compress under the weight and heat of the passing years, and thus, to become bedrock on which to build a future that fulfills my calling. For without reconciliation to the past that we have lost and left, we cannot take hold of that which is to come with alacrity and abandon. The most important life of all the lives that we have lived, is this life. The most important moment of this life is this moment.

It was in a later session with the Healer, when I was deeper still in hypnosis, that she bade me walk by creative visualisation upon a sea shore. I strolled along by the lapping waves, infusing the stillness of a fresh Spring morning and lost in the thoughts of a trance deeply enjoyed. A spaniel bounding playfully around me, nosing into driftwood and crabs with exuberant excitement. Then, I noticed, as the Healer correctly pointed out, there was someone walking towards me. Being too far away to see who it was initially, I continued in the direction of the figure, closing the gap between us, intrigued as to what was to happen. The Healer said she wasn't sure, but thought it might be a relative.

I was close enough now, to realise the form was familiar; yet, it was not so much the form, but rather, the presence that I sensed. I thought at first my grandfather was coming to impart some learning that it was time for me to be shown. It was a complete surprise to me to realise, when I drew close enough, that it was not my grandfather that approached me, but my grandmother.

I looked at her from afar. She was not the stooped and worn old person I had last known her as, but stood now in mature late middle age, perhaps, sixty years old. She was broader built than I recalled, but undeniably, it was her, and with a sense of spiritual awareness about her that she had never exhibited when I had known her.

In life, she had been a controlling, nagging manipulator, who had used and abused her loving husband mercilessly. He had been one of the most spiritually orientated people that I have ever been privileged to know. He would have had many lessons to teach me. Indeed, I have often felt his presence since he left, many years ago. But her? I found it hard to imagine there was anything of use that she could impart to me.

She spoke but a single sentence to me in measured tones of self-awareness and maturity. In that single statement, I sensed that she now spoke undeniably from the wisdom of spiritual awareness that she seemed never to have gained in her last lifetime. Her statement was this: "I have made my peace with him."

There was no more she needed to say. For at the speed of thought, I understood fully the implications of her words. In life, she had controlled, manipulated and sucked energy from him until the day he died an obscenely painful, cancerous death. She had lasted a further six years herself, her attention still lavished inexorably upon her own needs, oblivious to the capacity for caring and giving that she possessed, that we all possess. She was telling me now that she had been with him beyond the grave; that they were reconciled; that she had needed to pass through many lessons and made many mistakes; but also that he too had made his passage through this world in the manner he had planned before arriving in his last lifetime; that he had needed her for learning and growth as much as she had needed him.

But beyond this, a further awareness simultaneously came to me. For I also saw, that this was true not just of them, but also of me, and she who partnered me through the first half of my adult life. I saw that it is true of all of us. We come here, knowing the lessons we shall experience in growing towards maturity and ultimate enlightenment. We select the people that will be closest to us as we walk our journey through yet another lifetime; our parents, siblings, partners and teachers; our friends, lovers, abusers and betrayers. We derive learning through energy being dragged from us manipulatively, just as much as through it being graced to us in love. He could no more have completed his journey without her than she could have ended hers without him. They were interdependent, almost to the point of symbiosis.

I have repositioned her in my memory now. I have accorded her the place of honour that she deserves. I acknowledge too, my many other teachers in this lifetime, both temporal and spiritual. I am, who I am because of the fires I have passed through as much as because of the grace and indulgences heaped upon me. For though, I am very far from perfect, and though innumerable lessons remain for me yet, without both, I could not be who I am, where I am, what I am, ready to move into new learning; travelling new roads in the spirit and the flesh in the quest for growth and enlightenment. My future lies elsewhere that I would formerly have chosen, elsewhere that I had expected my past to dictate. I acknowledge with humble gratitude, the teachers and the lessons of my past. Having so acknowledged, I turn my eyes to the fore, to the educators and learnings, yet, to come. Thus, it is to walk in the spirit.

16. Servants of the Cause

Upon this day a thousand years ago
the azure sky to burning orange turned
when heart did clash on heart and steel on steel.
With anger thus congealed to human flesh
our generals of questionable cause
condemned a thousand thaumaturgic souls
upon the faintest flicker of a whim.

And was it on that day I crossed your sword
And looked into your fevered burning eyes
And smelled your ale-stale breath before my face
And named you in my anger "enemy"?

We sought to scale the castle keep that day
in unrepentant animated rage,
that you our holy cause would dare to thwart.
We hurled incessant barbs and F16s
as you defenders, burning oil did pour,
with mustard gas upon our rancid flesh,
and burnished tungsten naginatas drove,
full deep into our frightened, wavering souls.

So there and then I thrust my halberd forth
and sprayed my Tommy-gun across your heart
and wrenched your war torn soul from out your flesh.
Then at my own inevitable death
my enemy and I did grapple still,
like angry lovers locked in hate's embrace
your ectoplasm clawing at my shade
until Nirvana's mullahs spoke our names.

And did you stand that day for Genghis Kan
While under Hannibal I steadfast stood?
Or did you cry for Harry and his flag
While I allied myself to Franco's band?
What matters now the names for which we fought
when parliaments of reason silent stand
where numberless lost souls out-cry the cause?

We still storm castle walls in spirit form
where spectres of defenders pour the oil
that silently cascades to cliffs below.
Profligacy of death and wasted years
and endless squandered opportunities
cascade upon the ghost of reason's voice
and summon us to rise again to arms.

Forever shall we gather in this place
and in our "wisdom" conflict celebrate.
Another tankard shall we surely raise
that we might silence cries of misery
for loss of son, of father, spouse, of life.

Are we the damned?
Incarcerated souls?
Espoused to bellicose vocations we?
And shall we rise in human flesh once more
and march to future drums as yet unbeat?

No lessons have we learned at Freya's knee;
no wisdom have we gained from conflict's kiss;
nor shall, 'til we from Mars' service cease
for long enough to gaze on castle walls
and let our meditations light upon
the pansies and the peonies that grow
and tirelessly assault the crumbling lime
until the edifice is worn away.

And only then we Servants of the Cause
can lay aside our arms and humbly kneel,
and in such unfamiliar peace of mind
acknowledge Buddha nature in a flower.

17. Dreaming of Redlands

I'm sitting in my empty study on a bright sunny morning in April. The promise of spring is pouring through the window with the sunshine, making it difficult to read the words that even now are appearing on my screen. But there's another reason it's hard for me to see what I'm writing – my tears are obscuring my vision.

This gets me to thinking about all the other things we permit to obscure our vision. It is my observation, that we are most likely to get what we want and need from life, most likely to undertake successfully, the tasks we came here to fulfill, when we have clarity of vision. The Bible has it (and yes, I do quote from it a lot for someone who isn't a Christian) "Without a vision the people perish." The trouble is, that sometimes the vision becomes obscured and in extreme cases it gets lost altogether. It is my belief that such tasks and changes as we have come here to execute in ourselves that we do not fulfill in this lifetime, we simply have to return again in order to achieve on some future occasion. We come for growth and edification – of ourselves and of one another. To fulfill such aspirations of nobility requires an uncommon degree of focus on the vision we carried with us through our birth.

Yet, gradually, over the years, the visions can become obscured as the circumstances of the world in which we live take their toll. In this context, I observe in myself two sets of traits. Firstly, there are those that pertain to the vision, born of grace and characteristic of spiritual awareness, selfless and gentle, concerned for the long term welfare of those around me and those whose lives I touch. To the extent that I give myself to my vision of growth and edification, I energise both those around me and myself.

But I also note in myself another set of patterns that detract from the vision. The examples of these are many and varied, but seem to distill from two root causes. I find that if I give space in my thinking to ego needs or to fear, then, I am distracted from focussing on the light, from achieving that which I have come here to do. The patterns are generally unconscious, and all the more invidious for being so. Daily, I am confronted with challenges and opportunities of varying magnitude. In each case, I have the choice of addressing such circumstances either from the perspective of what I want to become, or what I once have been. I would wish my conscious choice always to be to move towards the vision of enlightenment and growth. But periodically, either innocently or deliberately, someone or something draws a knife across a nerve and I react.

We've all experienced it, of course. Perhaps, there is a put-down – some comment or act that is intended to make the initiating party feel superior at our expense. Or, perhaps, there is an attempt at manipulation – a seeking to gain some practical advantage at our cost. Then, it is we feel the old, old patterns begin to rise within us. "He can't speak to me like that!" Or "I'm not letting her get away with that!" The serpents of ego needs and the dragons of fear raise their heads from slumber and breath venom and fire into the identity of the erring party. To the extent that we are skilled in verbal assassination, the person concerned is diminished. Perhaps, they slink away, nursing broken pride and bruised in self-esteem, vowing vengeance upon us or some innocent third party. Or, perhaps, worse still, we are outgunned and we are the ones slinking away in shame, only to inflict pain on anyone unfortunate to cross our path that day. We nurture either the satisfaction or the pain of the encounter, depending on how it has gone for us. Either way, we carry the emotion of the event in our neurology where it combines with other similar experiences over long periods of time into gestalts of disharmony that distract us from our life contract.

Thus, we eventually come to run two opposing patterns in our minds and bodies; those that protect us with a view to preventing the world and the people around us from hurting us, and those that pertain to our vision of why we have come to walk upon the planet in the first place.

For my own part, my ego and fear patterns have run deep enough to dominate the first half of my life. It took an event of cataclysmic proportions to confront me with the knowledge that I had veered far off my intended path. I was, to all intents and purposes, walking in the opposite direction to that which served my long-term aims in this life time. But, I was blessed by those devastating experiences, for they have brought into consciousness, the patterns that hitherto were running outside of my awareness. Now, I am consistently more aware of the choices I face, both in daily dealings, and in decisions of long term and permanent importance. I can still continue to live my life in order to address ego needs and fear, if I wish to, of course. And in contemplating so doing, I am reminded of a phrase used by a wise friend of mine: "If you do what you always did, you'll get what you always got."

So, here I am, confronted with both choices, and an awareness of the fact that I can make those choices based on one of two sets of patterns that I run. If I want to, I can continue to address ego needs and fear. And, if I do so, I will fail to achieve the change and growth that I now regard as being the purpose for which I have entered this life. Or, alternatively, I can let go of old shibboleths and consciously choose not to look for safety and ego enhancement in my dealings. And the interesting thing is, when I do make my choices from the perspective of spiritual growth, I generally end up feeling both safer and more enhanced in my sense of self, anyway. These lessons are not easy, but we are wise to heed them diligently.

All this is tangential to the question of why I am unable to see the computer screen clearly, this morning, for cause of tears in my eyes. I think that the most accurate answer to that question, though not the most succinct, is that, it is not only ego needs and fears that obscure our vision – it is dreams as well.

It seems to me that if I hold what I refer to as a vision, it is selfless. It grows in my heart from the tiniest of seeds, until, if I will permit it, it encompasses the breadth and depth and length and height of my capacity to achieve growth and edification in the world. It becomes a consuming passion, burning up self-interest in the intensity of the selflessness intrinsic to the vocation. If you are fortunate enough to hold fast in your heart such a vision, you are blessed indeed. But also acknowledge that its overriding characteristic is that you do not hold it exclusively for your own benefit. Rather, understand that it is sustained and nurtured on the energy of spirit for the wider edification and the achievement of the mission you came here to fulfill.

By contrast, a dream, as I define it, always seems to have "me" at the centre of it. I visualise myself in some state, different from that in which I now find myself, that enhances a self-aggrandised representation of me for the benefit of me. Certainly, the dream includes other dramatis personae, but always, it seems to have me at the centre. I observe, to my discredit, that I have held such dreams close to my heart for most of my life.

I have heard it said that we should take great care over the dreams we dream, lest we find they become our reality. I am a living testimony to the fact that they do, for the ultimate representation I dreamed for me and mine was to make millions and live a country lifestyle, with pool parties and paddocks and ponies for the children. Well, by stripping my attention and energy away from everything that really mattered, eventually, I achieved my dream, and here I am sitting at my desk in my study in a country house called Redlands. The problem was that, I discovered too late that the dream was not shared by my children, who were now too old to want ponies and paddocks, and by my wife who sought fulfillment in dreams of her own. And in addition, I found that dreams once fulfilled by the exclusion of all other considerations have to be sustained by the same level of energy and exclusivity. I had promised myself a life of ease once I had accumulated sufficient wealth, once the dream had been achieved. But, the price had been too high. My children had grown and my wife had drifted away from me in frustration at my obsession. She left last year and I shall leave in less than forty-eight hours. The boxes are packed, the rooms silent and echoing. I said goodbye to my history some days ago. I took pictures inside and out, and I hugged some of the trees. I sold off the garden equipment that I will no longer need and split the furniture with she who shares my past.

I hold now to the vision of a future devoted to a vocation, for without a vision, the people do indeed perish. And I know now so very clearly the difference between dreams and visions. The price of learning has been immeasurable.

18. Resentment

In long dark nights of savoured animosity
he came to her;
and lustful in outpourings of acidity
without consent
did cast himself in violence on her flesh,
'til she neared suffocation from incessant taunts
and fought for breath as bitterness did sorely seek
to crush her spirit's impuissant bones.

And so it was in incandescent arrogance,
for other cause than present deeds portrayed,
he thrust snide barbs of phallic hate's ejaculate
and flooded her identity
with putrid seeds of self-destructive doubt.

He that should return but love to charity
with vile sarcastic bounty showered her then;
and tokens of malevolent intolerance
that froze to stone her passion's molten core,
so sharp the crafted barbs of hate bestowed.

She thought her destiny to cede her life that night.
but in surprise outlived invective's flood.
Communion did she take then with the
                                    immanence
and bonded to an unborn child within.

Through months of introspective animosity
each parent did with malice taunt their spouse
and thus her husband did in hate encourage her
to nurture foetal loathing in her flesh.

Then after full gestation unto term it came
as waters of her tears discharged in floods.
She knew her time was nigh unto delivery.
As tempests raged, within, and raged without,
disgorged she from her flesh the child of enmity
that sucked upon the substance of her soul.

Then looked they on the spawn of their identity
which twisted and deformed from out her leapt,
repugnant progeny of shared antipathy,
and each indulged in proud parental joy
that such a one as this they could call 'son.'

They gazed with love upon the malformed entity,
and when the child looked up into their eyes,
and with familial loathing sought their souls to
                                    gouge,
then knew they, they would love it all their days.

For hours on end they gave their thoughts in
                                    probity
to questions of the baby's given name;
considered 'Anguish,' 'Passion,' 'Rage,' but
                                    thought none apt.
And for his part the father wished 'Depravity,'
but settled she upon the name
'Resentment.'

To nurturing Resentment she did give her life,
And stopping up her ears to other calls,
With crafted hate did exorcise from out her heart
distractions of forgiveness and of charity
and thus obsesssed she chose to spend her days.

Her personal potential gladly laid she down
in favour of a single better cause:
and greatness forced upon the wizened child.

The father too did play a parent's proper part
and laboured in devotions of his own
to bring about Resentment's full development.

Thus daily they would shriek their case to greater
                                    right
unto the child that they had jointly spawned.

She cosseted and fed her hungry progeny.
In clothes of righteous anger she him dressed.
A tutor did she hire named Consanguinity,
and no expense was spared till he did supplicate
in vindication's graduation robes.

And so the inexcusable malignancy
of their exquisite hate did greater grow.

And when he came at last to full maturity,
he showed he had imbibed his lessons well.
He demonstrated all the careful nurturing
that had been lavished on him was worthwhile.

For as his parents vented animosity,
he reached into the kitchen drawer one day
and boldly took to him the knife of bitterness.
Then as he slit his parents' hearts from out their
                                                    breasts,
they smiled on him with deep parental pride
that long indulgent years of breeding enmity
had reached to such fruition in their flesh.

19. Do Not Go Gentle

I really thought you were going to die today. I watched you cross the restaurant without lifting your feet from the floor. Peter supported you on one arm, Rachel on the other. I think for the first time in all the years I have known you, I saw fear upon your face; and relief, such unutterable relief as you finally made it to the table and sank gratefully into your chair.

I know now that your most important value has always been to be in control. Strange that I never saw it before, since being in control is so important to me. Maybe, it was the first lesson you ever taught me. Over the last 18 months, little by little, your control has slipped away. Today, I finally watched you shed it like a discarded snakeskin. The new reality emerged: old, frail, and now finally admitting that Parkinson's has taken control of you. Today, you gave up the fight.

I sat across the same table from you, hating to be confronted with the reality of human decline. Physical and mental, it bestows itself upon us, unbidden, like some macabre Yuletide gift as we enter the final phase. It sits upon our lap with its fascinating wrapping and tempts us to open it. And open it we must. We delve into it to find what it is that

Santa has brought us. Now you really understand the meaning of the gift you have been brought.

You are an enigma. You raise so many issues for me when I see you like this. When you were fit and healthy, I could be angry with you. I could run movies in my mind of the day that I would tell you of the pain that you had caused, finally, allowing me to exorcise my ghosts. I could revert into inner child and roar my rage for the frustration, the endless frustration of ever being bent to your will. For when I was a child, I thought as a child, I spoke as a child; but you could never put away childish things. And the anger I carry for incessant violations of my identity still resonates down the decades. There is pain in my heart even now.

But now, I cannot tell you. For what you have become confronts me with what I have become. And the values you have instilled in me make me realise that there is no point in tormenting you with your foolishness in these closing moments of the final act before the curtain falls for the last time. So, I will continue to carry silently what I have carried silently all these years. You win again. You have created your child in your own image.

We never do seek to create our children in our own image, do we? We hope to create them in the image of what we wish we had been, and thus, to live vicariously. Who is the parent amongst us who has not sought to nurture in the child, that, which they value most dearly? Even the most neglectful communicate their highest value of selfish disinterest to their children by their absence. Perhaps, we do get the children we deserve. Perhaps, you deserve me.

I have learned so much of life from you. Whether you consciously intended to teach me, I doubt. But as the Taoist has it, "There is a way of being in the world where the teachers teach without teaching and the learners learn without learning." And it is, thus, that you have taught me how to be and how not to be. And, if I have learned a little from you, then, I am grateful, for I never understood that you were my teacher.

That which I did learn, I did not learn consciously. I infused it, day after day, year after year by observation of repeated patterns. This was the learning that you could not know you had. This was the inheritance that I did not know I had already received. For your way of being has become, in part, my way of being. So very much, do I see in you, that I am afraid is true of me. So very much, do I see in you, that I am afraid will never be true of me.

We took you back from the restaurant to the care home. We laid you on your bed. We called the doctor to you. We did all the right and proper things. And then, we went home and waited. And in the night, I thought of you. I wondered, what was my earliest memory of you? When did you loom into my life? I can remember a shadowy, remote figure who would bring me chocolate at the end of his working day. And I can remember my incessant three-year-old's question, as you walked in the door each evening and as I made a bee-line straight for your briefcase, and asked "What have you got for me?" You know, I don't think I've ever stopped asking you that question. I rather think, that none of us ever stops asking it of our parents. I ask you in the recesses of my mind, every time I come to talk there with you. It is still a child's question. It is still a selfish question. The fact that I feel it so, is part of the learning that I have learned without learning.

When was it, I wonder, that I began to be aware of the substance that you had? There was a time, sometime, when I reframed you in my mind. Until then, I really thought I had you clear. My conscious opinion of you was low. You had so very little that I wanted and even less to teach me. But at some point, and I really can't remember when, now, I finally began to get a handle on the choices you had made. And choices are the one thing we all have in common. You chose to live with responsibility. Once upon a time, for whatever reason, you had taken responsibility for another person. As a consequence of that, you took responsibility for us, your children. Many times I wondered why you had not left. But I eventually came to realise that you were an old army man, and no deserter; that having made your choice, you set your face to live with it, regardless of the consequences.

When dawn touched the treetops, I rose. Silently, I crunched my way down the gravel drive and slipped silently into the forest. The dryads did not crowd me. They remain at a respectful distance when a passing is nigh.

Funny, isn't it, what comes to mind when you're alone and you don't try to control your thoughts. I travelled back to 1987, that dawn. I was thirty years old, in my first maturity... the one where you think you have finally grown up, but you still don't realise how much there is still to learn ahead of you. I was to have a political career. I was a candidate in the parliamentary election that year. You never shared my political convictions of the day (neither do I now). Yet, when you knew what I was doing, you dropped everything and came to help. You sought no glory or even recognition. You sat silently at a table and for three weeks addressed envelopes for a mailing. Boring, mind-numbing work; you did it for me. You did it to tell me something you were never able to articulate; something that even now, I'm not quite ready to say to you, or for you, or of you. Give me a little more time,

Dad. I'm nearly there. I can almost say it. Read to the end and I think I'll have it for you by the time you finish.

I wish I could be noble about this, Dad. I wish I could tell you what a wonderful relationship we had. I wish I could tell you that you were Superman. But you weren't, and I'm not. Maybe, we are not adults ourselves until we finally grasp that our parents were neither all good nor all bad; that like us, they held their fragile humanity, tenuously balancing their patterns and ever asking their deity, "Why hast Thou made me thus?"

And now, when there is so very little time left, perhaps, I have begun to learn who you really are. We will never discuss this, for your ability to speak is almost gone: one of the earlier casualties of the Parkinson's. And my ability to hear is almost gone, a casualty of who knows what? So, we sit across the table set between us, laden with sustenance that would satisfy us both. And we do not sup. We continue to be, as we always have been. We communicate with few words, superficially. For even now, I cannot pluck up the courage to reach out and touch you. There is so much that can never be articulated now. There are so many explanations that will never be made. So many reasons for the things that we both did and did not do, that no longer matter in themselves. They matter only insofar as they contribute to the undisturbed banquet that will remain before us, until you finally rise from the table.

And when that time comes, I will still not have learned without learning, all that you have to teach without teaching. I will continue to sit and ponder on the meaning of the banquet before me. Then, within the deep internal recesses where I keep the real you, I shall continue to listen to the things you never said. I shall be grateful for the unanswered questions, for I know now, that questions open, whereas answers merely close. Perhaps, you really did mean to teach me this. How very well you have made me in your own image.

If I have learned to value anything in myself, it is the insatiable desire I carry to learn and to grow and to become wise. I still mock my own foolishness. I still hate my own weakness. I still wish that I was more than I am and more than I will ever be. So well have I learned my lessons without learning and taken the teaching the you have taught without teaching.

I know that soon, now, you will go gently. It has never been your way to rage. And you will not rage now at the dying of the light. You will not lift up your voice and howl at the moon to mark your passing. You will not be heard. Your rising from the table will be as unassuming as your presence there ever was.

Then, when you are done; when the rituals are done; when they have fussed over your shell to their hearts' content; when they have cried their tears; when they have expressed all they need to express in all the ways they need to express it; then, it is, that you and I shall rise from the table and take our leave.

We shall walk within the forest. For we never did. We shall choose each other's company. For we never did. We shall stand in the storms together. For we never did. We shall withstand the world together. For we never did. We shall discourse deep unto deep. For we never did. We shall, each of us, hold the heart of the other. For we never did. We shall, each of us, see the soul of the other. For we never did.

And once, just once, we shall each of us say unto the other, "I love you."

For we never did.

20. A Love Less Ordinary

She is no ordinary lover;
for no discrimination turns her heart.
And no respecter, thus, of persons, she
will welcome high and low born to her arms:
men of mettle, men of grace,
men of justice, men of sin,
men of truth she will embrace
and no morality prefer,
for ultimately all fall to her charms.

She is no ordinary lover.
See, some in wanton folly to her flee.
They seek a fabricated immortality
in fleeting memories of son's sons.
Impermanence eternal would they hope to make
by raising transient monoliths,
and writing names in obelisks,
corrupted, passing edifice,
that carves no lasting gain into their souls.

She is no ordinary lover
Still others flee her charms and gentle touch
postponing their appointed time to wed.
In patience no frustration will she show
as lovers soil themselves and fornicate
with deeds that time alone appropriates.
They would procrastinate for evermore,
eternal growth eternally postpone,
until she reads predestination's bands.

She is no ordinary lover.
In folly, too, I sought to make my mark
indelible on sea-washed golden sands
of kingdoms, merely temporal,
ethereal, ephemeral,
until at last I learned
that my appointed task
was not to leave my mark upon the world,
but rather, let it carve its wisdom on my soul.

She is no ordinary lover.
She silent bides and will her own time take
that when your learning is enough,
and you have lately come to know
that learning's only proper end
is your own self and heart to understand,
then in her own time she'll call you.
That final approbation you should seek
within the pure caresses of her lips.

She is no ordinary lover.
Her cool caress shall hold no fear for you
when in due time the end of learning comes.
And at the time she summons you,
forsaking all others
will you cleave only unto her
as long as you both shall
both shall…
both shall…

21. In Sure Uncertain Hope

It's 10.15 pm, Sunday 7th July 2002. The phone rings. It's the nurse at the nursing home. "Hello Mr. Forester. I wanted to tell you, your father is *very* poorly." She emphasises the word very. It's medical euphemism speak. I'm a layman in a hurry. There is no space in my vocabulary for sensibilities. I need to clarify. I say "Thank you, nurse. I need to understand what you're saying. You're telling me he's dying and I should come and be with him until he's gone, yes?

There is a pause at the other end of the line while she switches modes to adjust to my bluntness. Once more, I observe silently that the medical fraternity feels uncomfortable when you ask them to step across the boundaries of professionalism. I am stripping her of the comfort of gentle words for the sake of jagged edged clarity. "Yes" she finally answers. I ask if she's informed my brother, ascertain that she has not and step immediately into action. Action is my own reflex response. Action is where I feel comfortable. Action softens the jagged edges of the emotional precipice I am beginning to peer over. Doing something, anything is where I feel most comfortable, safest. It is my way of avoiding the emotional vertigo induced by the sight of the drop over the edge. I call my brother Peter and appraise him. He says he'll come from London now. He asks me to call Mum's care home – I stop, my emotional autopilot momentarily confused between the need for speed induced by the obligation I feel to my father, and my intuitive childhood pattern to comply with the request of my older brother. I stay in indecision until adult rationality kicks back in again and I ask him to do it himself as I'm in a hurry. He agrees, grateful for this moment to be told what to do; and I feel a little less controlled. He doesn't mean it as control. Is it the lifelong lot of the younger to feel that any request from the elder is a control act? There's no time for sibling rivalry now – or philosophy.

I step into the shower, conscious that I am at that moment beginning to break new ground. I am adjusting to the grown up responsibility of attending my father's passing. I am aware, almost as if floating above myself, of the merging of my inner child and adult. I am in crash course preparation for the emotional energy drain that will be required of me by the forthcoming management of my father's passing and the covert rituals, we, as a family will employ. I feel strangely mature as I rise to the task. My inner-ten-year old is silent. The sun is in Gemini and my adult is in the ascendant.

On the way to the nursing home I check that my mother's taxi has been called and I phone Natalie, my elder daughter. I get the answer phone – she's gone to church. I leave a message. That's all the action taken that needs to be taken. I head on out to my 10.30 appointment with karma.

I arrive at the nursing home. The surroundings are normal. It is only I, who am different: confident, assertive in taking control, knowing that I am about to step over the self-imposed boundary that I have erected, God knows how many years ago. I am acutely aware that in an overt act of compassion, I am shortly to touch my father, adult to adult, my strong to his weak, openly and honestly for the first and last time in my life.

The nurse meets me, accompanies me to his room. They have his stereo playing classical music softly – Maria Callas sings operatic aria that drip-feed emotion into an already charged atmosphere. He hears the music. Hearing is the last sense to go, they tell me. He's in the bed awake, not sleeping as I had anticipated. It's 10.30 and it's going to be an hour before my mother arrives and several more before Peter comes. I have him to myself for a while –for long enough to say what needs to pass between us. And as I look down on his contracted, emaciated frame, his upper lip folded over his lower jaw and his frightened eyes, I know, I can allow myself to love my father openly for the last time – almost for the first time. I smile as I sit down. Is it truly the first time I have been in his presence without fear; the first time I have felt no need for restraint?

"Hello Dad, it's Michael." I reach out my hand and place it lightly over his, the bed sheet separating us from actual physical contact. I can't, yet, bring myself to touch him flesh to flesh. "I'm here now and I'm not going away until you're ready." It's a rash promise that later in the day, I will break, but neither of us knows that, at this moment. I'm expecting him to die within minutes. "I'm glad we're alone," I continue, "glad to have you to myself for a while." The words are those that occur to me moment by moment. They come sporadically, like water gushing in uneven bursts from an air contaminated tap. Disjointed phrases and sentences bubble up intermittently as I release the padlocks on the metal bands that I have wrapped around my chest, to constrain my heart from telling him, how I see it all for so many years. It is almost, as if, I am exhaling spiritually for the first time in my life.

"I want you to know, I love you, Dad." The words that used to be so hard, used to be beyond my capacity to utter, now come effortlessly. Maybe, it's because he can't reply, maybe, because it's the last chance I'll get to tell him, and I'm determined not to let the opportunity pass. He looks up at me through half closed eyes, tries to free his hands from the bed clothes, tries to speak. "You don't need to say anything, Dad, and you don't need to do anything." I am smiling softly at him and the tears are beginning to roll gently from my eyes. The possibility of these tears being seen by him or anyone else are positively the last thing I care about at this moment. "Everything you ever needed to do has been done. All you need now is to be who you are. The effort is over. It is enough." He continues to try to speak. Simply 'being' doesn't come easily to him. "Mum and Peter are on their way, but you don't need to wait for them if you're ready to go." I know he won't. He will be feeling an obligation to hang on until they come. He has lived for obligation and will not change now. "You go in your own time dad. The work's all done and you've done very, very well." My heart is speaking words of gentle softness, my only focus, to give him what he needs to ease his transition. "I want you to know how well you've done and that I'm proud you're my father."

My tears are coming faster now. The nurse comes in and looks at him, looks at me. I don't mind if she sees my crying. I'm proud to love this man, this wizened, emaciated bag of bones within which dwells the spirit of my father for a little longer yet. She places a hand on my shoulder for a moment and smiles. She leaves, a blur of blue uniform gliding wordlessly out of the open door. These amazing people, poorly paid and proud servants of a vocation to ease the last days of the dying, will be in and out in this fashion all day long, offering tea and sandwiches and gentleness and grace in whatever measure is required at whatever time, the silent heroes and heroines of our passing hours.

The room fades again. There is only him and me. "I don't think I've ever told you I'm proud of you, Dad," I continue. "Never told you how grateful I am for what you did – or more for what you didn't do. You didn't leave, Dad. You stayed with her and with us. Must have been many, many occasions on which you wanted to go. But you stayed the course for our sakes. That's an incredible achievement, and I want you to know how grateful I am that you did it." I can see it clearly now, for the first time; the impact of his fulfillment of his own life contract upon my ability to undertake mine. I am aware that our shared being has been about something completely different from that which I have previously thought. This moment is in itself a rite of passage, marking my transition from one level of awareness to another. It is the final coming of adulthood in the soft amber glow of my father's imminent passing. Now, I am seeing purpose, method, structure in the construct of our lives that I have never been conscious of before. Representations of randomness that have surrounded my clouded thinking are at this moment giving way to perceptions of the purpose, the pre life choices, the karma that governs all our lives. "Because you did what you came to do," I continue, "you've enabled me to become who I needed to be, so that I could do what I came to do. I couldn't have done it without you, Dad. I owe you a lot and I'm grateful."

He looks up at me and tries to speak again, his eyes widening and his arm moving in a fruitless attempt to convey what he wants to say. If you are a person who can see auras, at this moment you would observe mine feeding energy to his in truckloads. I know I will finish the day exhausted, and I don't give a damn. I know what he wants to say but cannot, so I'll say it for him. "I know what you want to say, Dad, " I continue. "You want to talk of obligation and the meeting of someone else's needs. But you don't have to say anything, and you don't have to do anything. And Dad, I'm glad to be able to show you who I really am at last. I know who you are now, and I'm glad to show you who I am inside." My words slow again. I let them ebb and flow at their own pace. Words mined from the gold seams of the heart are not for the rushing. "I won't be able to do this when they come," I continue. I'll feel intimidated again and wrap myself in the shroud of effacement I usually show the world. But you know different now, Dad. You know who I really am." I smile at him, the tears still falling.

I watch him as he moves his mouth, still trying to speak, moves his hands to extricate himself from the bed clothes. I'm ready to touch him now. I ease back the top sheet from the skin and bone that is all that's left of his arm and marvel at the physical deterioration that we undergo at the end of our lives. How is it possible still to live when so little of your life force remains? It will not be long now. I reach out my hand and gently caress his arm, touch my healthy flesh to his dying flesh, my vibrant energy to his fading energy. I imagine Mr. Parkinson, ethereal spectre of the sufferers of Parkinson's disease and younger brother to the Grim Reaper, standing silently in the corner of the room. Dressed in pinstripes and an open-neck white shirt, he leans nonchalantly against the window ledge, hands in pockets, biding his time and watching us. He will know when it's his turn to take centre stage. He carries no scythe like that of his elder sibling. The tools of his trade are the wizening wand and the noose rope. He has caressed this man's flesh with the former for many, many months now, emaciating him meticulously, jolting and lurching him uncomfortably towards an undignified end that my father even now manages to out run for a little longer. He has finished with the wand now. Shortly, he will take his rope and wind it round my father's throat one final time, constricting the life out of him. But for now, Mr. Parkinson is content to watch us a little longer as I look into Dad's eyes and stroke his arm, listening to his rattling breath coming ever shorter, ever shallower.

My words continue sporadically. "Work's all done now, Dad," I say reassuringly. "You can take your leave whenever you're ready. And until it's time to go, all you need to do is be." Something about this time is tapping deep into me in a way few external events have ever done. I am talking spirit to spirit now, as I have never done with him before, at least in this life time. I speak the words as they come into my mind, uncertain, even as I say them, as to whether they are wholly wise, whether they fit his conception of reality. But they are the only words that come, the only gift I have to lay as a burnt offering upon his altar this final time. "When you're ready to go, they'll be waiting for you, Dad. Your own mother and father are on the other side waiting to meet you." Is this fanciful? I don't think so. I'm speaking the words as they are appearing in my mind. It feels like I'm a messenger, delivering what he needs to hear. "I love you, Dad," I reassure him again. The shallow, rattling breathing continues. Then, without warning, my mother walks into the room. Our time of shared solitude in the antechamber of silence is over, and I feel my true identity slip back under the waves of protective super ego that I have long since cultivated to feel safe around my family. I smile at him and stroke his hand once more, then vacate the chair so that she can sit by him dutifully. Maria Callas continues to weep arias in bucket loads from the stereo.

All that day, we sit with him. I do not try to speak with him again. Peter arrives and I go off for some brief respite, aware that I'm breaking the promise I made him earlier. I don't think he'll mind. I head for the supermarket and the Sunday papers. I sip an orange juice in the café for a few moments, watching the routines of daily living tumble chaotically around me. The normality is surreal. I take the papers back to the nursing home where we three sit silently around the bed. I read, glancing at him every few minutes, assessing his breathing and gently stroking his arm when he seems disturbed. Mozart and Bach share our sentry duty. My mother's words and attention are for the composers, not for the man in the bed, as she avoids the reality of his passing a little longer. I want to comment but refrain. The atmosphere is peaceful, churchlike. The angels of the nursing home, cleaners and care assistants, cooks and nurses, glide silently in and out of the room, smiling gently to acknowledge the passing of this man they have come to love and respect, proffering more tea and gentleness. We try to work out what constitutes appropriate behaviour in circumstances with which none of us is familiar.

Isobel Allende's book, "Paula," is on my mind. I recall that she writes of the passing of her daughter; how her relatives, both the living and the dead, congregate in the room as Paula's moment of transition approaches. We, the living, are assembled. I await the coming of the dead in futility. Perhaps, it is too soon. Perhaps, they will come nearer the time of crossing over. Perhaps, they are here already and I am not sensitive enough to be aware of them. Perhaps, they are not coming. Perhaps, there is no "sure and certain hope of the resurrection." Perhaps, all flesh simply is like grass and upon death we cease to be. Perhaps. Perhaps. Perhaps.

The hours creep on and his breathing grows more shallow.

7.30 p.m. arrives and with it the change of staff shift. A dilemma presents itself. Do we stay indefinitely or do we take mother home? Though Dad's breathing grows ever more shallow, we opt for the latter on the grounds that the staff will sit with him through the night. We drop her off at her care home and head into Lymington for a meal. I share a private time with Peter, groping my way towards a relative intimacy that is as yet alien to me. Perhaps, it is to him too, but he seems readier for it than I. Moules Marinaire and parsnip soup seem a surreal way to spend the evening of the day we have shared. I look around the small restaurant at half a dozen tables filled with couples of varying ages. I notice the young couple sitting by the mirror, eyes only for each other. I remember being like that myself once. I feel my isolation.

Peter's mobile phone rings as we eat. Mother's care home advises us that there will be no taxi in the night to take mum to the nursing home should she need to go. We work out a strategy to get her to his bedside as quickly as possible in the event that it proves necessary. A middle-aged man at the next table to us mutters in irritation at people taking phone calls in restaurants. My brother catches his attention and explains the circumstances. He is still unmoved. We have disturbed him, and we ought to know better. Self-justification takes no prisoners. There is a groundswell of quiet support for us in the restaurant as other diners line up emotionally behind us. In embarrassment the irate man recedes silently into himself. We pay and leave, our machine-gun nests of righteousness still holding the moral high ground. We head for home and an exhausted bed, anticipating a phone call from the nursing home in the night. I am amazed he has lasted as long as he has. 3.00 a.m. arrives and I wake, though not because of some dramatic premonition that this is the time. I simply cannot sleep, head for the computer and write up the day's events. We are all prone to seeking security in the habitual at times of acute stress.

At 4.30 am, I phone the home. "His pulse is down to thirty-three" says the night nurse. The information means little to me but she conveys all I need to know in her tone of voice. It is clear that he is not expected to last much longer. I ask if we should come now. I'm told not to, as his pulse could well pick up again. I kill time until 8.30 arrives and we leave to collect mother. The trip to her care home and then with her to Dad's nursing home has taken on the sense of macabre familiarity. I'm very, very tired already, and there is another draining day of sitting and waiting ahead.

We arrive to the news that there is no change and settle into our now familiar chairs, still set out around his bed as we left them the previous night. The night staff have sat with him all through the dark hours so that he will not be alone in the event that death comes suddenly. I imbibe again the sense of how special these people are, those that carry the vocation of nursing the dying. Day to day their quiet heroism goes unapplauded as they proceed unassumingly with the routines of cleaning, coffee making or washing patients. But when a passing is nigh each of them seems to take on an other worldly quality as they beam energy to the one that is shortly to depart. As person after person calls into his room to see how he is doing, I see the same light in their eyes. I can all but reach out and touch the energy they send towards him, not to keep him alive, but rather to ease his passage from the body. I am overflowing with admiration for these people who touch soul reality on a daily basis in a way that I can only begin to grasp at.

It is to be a war of attrition now, and the victor and the vanquished are already known. That cool dude, Mr. Parkinson, glides back into the room in his pin stripes. He takes up his familiar position at the window and leans back, one black lace-up shoe crossed over the other as he bides his time until the final telegram comes with instructions for him to dispatch another victim. Give me the hooded Reaper with his scythe any day. This guy seems to enjoy his task far too much for my liking. My attention returns to the room. In reality, I am not a seer of spirits. For me, there are only we three living visitors in our chairs and one barely surviving patient on the bed.

I look at my father differently now, counting his breaths as I surreptitiously eye the second hand of my watch. About one breath per second, I calculate over a quarter of a minute. Slow, rasping breaths dragging teaspoons of air into his lungs. I wonder how many more he will have the strength to take before he gives up. He is somehow my father and not my father all at once. He is still someone I care for still, but he is difficult to equate with the man I have known in strength and weakness over my forty six years.

I have brought books to read and papers to write on this time. I don't want another day as empty as yesterday. So I read essays about John Steinbeck and "East of Eden" and I rewrite the synopsis for my own novel that I secretly and naively hope that will somehow echo the greatness of the work of my writer-hero.

As the day proceeds, I take periodic glances across the room to the bed, looking for some minute change in him. I perceive none. He continues to rasp his way through the day, his fingernails barely gripping onto the sheer rock face of physical life. At intervals, the nurses shoo us from the room while they turn him or wash him. We are grateful for the obligation to leave, and take breaks that grow longer and longer. We are all emotionally exhausted, and with each withdrawal from our vigil, we grow more and more reluctant to return.

After a lunch that is longer than it needs to be or than it reasonably ought to be under the circumstances, we return to the room once more and ease our shoulders back into the afternoon's work.

God help me, I am wishing for the hastening of his departure as much for my own sake as for his, if not more. I don't want to watch this any longer. I don't want to listen to the rattling breaths. I don't want to see him with his mouth open, lips sweating as he gulps for air, still clinging onto life. I don't want to sit here wondering what to do and where to look. But I do all these things and I know, I learn and grow and walk my own karma with every moment that passes. My education continues.

At 3.00 pm, the doctor comes and we are shepherded from the room once more. He emerges a few minutes later, looking predictably grave. He mumbles something about Dad's body shutting down. He can give us no indication of how long it will take. The medical fraternity is understandably unwilling to go on record with promises of time scales, they themselves cannot accurately estimate. A family conference results in our deciding to disperse, since we have no way of knowing how long the end will be in coming. As I exit the care home, matron calls me aside. Without actually using the words of commitment, she manages to convey to me that she thinks, it cannot be much longer. I gather that in effect, I'm being told it's going to be today. I head for home. It's going to be a long night. Whether it's a short night or a long night, it's going to be a long, long night.

I read over what I've typed above and look at the clock. It's 9.30 pm. I decide to phone the nursing home and check on how he's doing. The care assistant says there's been no change and they'll call when something happens. I get myself ready for bed. Half an hour later the phone rings again. The nurse in charge is worried. He's deteriorating and I should come. "Do I have time to collect my mother?" I enquire. "It will take me about an hour to get to Dad if I do." The nurse thinks that's ok. Two minutes later as I'm getting back into my day clothes the phone rings again. It's the nurse. "I'm sorry, Michael. He's gone."

As is my way of dealing with emotion initially, I do not give myself time to react. I phone Peter before I leave, and Natalie, as I walk out of the door. I make a conscious choice not to phone Mum. I will tell her face to face. In the car, I phone my younger daughter and ex-wife, but apparently, they are not back in the country yet. I leave an answer phone message. My mind is active as I drive out to collect Mum, filled with all the practical matters of funeral directors and death certificates, wills and pensions. Then, I am aware of my distractive thinking receding, and I allow myself to realise for the first time that my father is dead. It seems strange as I say it to myself – so normal in the way of the world, yet, so alien to my personal experience. My father has never been dead before. It will take some getting used to.

I arrive at Mum's and tell her as gently as possible that he's gone. She reacts emotionally for the first time and cries. When she is composed, I drive her to the nursing home where the night nurse meets us and shows us into Dad's room. The sheet is pulled up over him. I am uncomfortable at the prospect of seeing a lifeless body for the first time in my life. But he looks the same as he did when I saw him last, except that the look of struggle is gone from him now. And with it, he seems to have grown larger again. Perhaps it's a trick of the light, but he definitely looks more substantial now, than he did seven hours ago. The nurse withdraws and we sit quietly. I ask my mother if she wants me to leave. She says "not yet" and we continue in silence. Then, she surprises me. "Would it embarrass you if I said a little prayer?" she asks.

"Not at all," I reply confidently, embarrassed already. She begins to pray; for us to have the strength to continue without him; for him to be happy and safe. I guess I shouldn't be surprised. I knew the rewriting of history would begin immediately.

She leaves the room momentarily and I feel uncomfortable there on my own. And I do, indeed, feel I am on my own, for I feel no other life force in there with me. Try as I might, I get no sense of his presence. Having struggled to stay so long, it is evident that once free of the flesh, he has taken his leave quickly, leaving no lingering sense of his presence. Either that, or my aura is made of lead. She returns to the room and I leave for a while to allow her some time alone with him.

After a decent interval, I return and tell her its time for me to take her home. She exits the room again for the last time, and I am again alone with him momentarily. I will not leave him uncovered. I move towards the bed and reach for the sheet. As I pull it up over his face I smile down at him. "Goodbye Dad," I whisper. "See you again soon."

22. Oh My God

"Repent!" Shouted the man with the big black bible and the floppy hat.

I didn't know what penting was, let alone re-penting.

"All ye like sheep have gone astray," he said, "and wandered to his own way."

I thought of new season's lamb with mint sauce and roast potatoes and...

" Repent for the kingdom of heaven is at hand," he said, glaring down at me with menacing eyes.

I looked at my hands but I couldn't see anything that looked like a kingdom.

"I see you, sinner," he said.

I felt guilty.

"Repent, he said again. "For the Kingdom of Heaven comes like a thief in the night and no one shall be warned of its coming."

I made a mental note to lock the front door before it got dark.

"There will be weeping and wailing and gnashing of teeth," he said.

I wiped tear from my eye and adjusted my dentures.

"What is your god?" he demanded of me in a booming voice.

Everyone turned to look at me.

So I had to answer, didn't I?
So I looked at him.
And said

My God's the one that sweats blood in a lonely garden.
My God's the one carrying a cross up a hill on his back.
My God's the one with twelve inch thorns crush down onto
    his head.
My God's the one stripped naked and nailed up high.
My God's the one who forgives thieves.
My God's the one whose body burned its way through a
    winding sheet.
My God's the one that Death wasn't strong enough to hold
    (and believe me, Death's pretty pissed off about that).
My God's the one who kicked an 'effin great boulder out of
    his way and strode out of a tomb.
My God's the one who forgave every bad or stupid thing I
    ever did.
And He doesn't give a toss what anyone else thinks of me.

That's my God, I said. So tell me,
What's yours like?

23. Keeping my sword hand free

I am sometimes asked by my American friends, why it is that, whereas the rest of the civilised world chooses to drive on the right-hand side of the road, the UK and nations historically influenced by the UK prefer to drive on the left. Now, it may be that the answer to this question is simply that we are awkward and that we find our identity in being different. However, there is, as I understand it, a historical explanation as well. We are an old nation and, being bounded by the seas, guard jealously our sense of security. It is therefore, perhaps, hardly surprising that we deem our safety to be of paramount importance to us. I am told that this rather eccentric habit of driving on the wrong side of the road actually originates with that need to feel safe.

To understand this, you have to go back to the era of knights in shining armour. In days of old, the alpha males of the land would seek to demonstrate their superiority over one another in mock combat. In particular, jousting tournaments would be held. Knights would charge towards each other resplendent in full regalia, colours flying, lances at the ready, each with the avowed intent of knocking the other from the horse and battling close to, but not quite up to the point of death.

Now, naturally, such a procedure requires some reasonably standard rules of engagement. One of these, I am reliably informed (and it's pretty obvious when you think about it), was that, you would pass lance to lance. The majority of the population being right-handed, this implied that you would pass your opponent on the left side. Passing on the left kept your lance arm and your sword hand readily available to engage in combat. This, then, was the agreed methodology by which you would seek to beat the living daylights out of your opponent. If successful, you could consider yourself a cool dude and fair maidens would fall in swoons at your feet.

What you were supposed to do, if like me, you were left-handed, I have never quite been able to establish. No doubt, if such politically incorrect and barbaric competitions were to take place in our age, there would be some public body charged with responsibility for ensuring that the manually-challenged such as I, were not excluded from our legitimate entitlement to participate equally alongside our right-handed fellow citizens (who, it would be recognised – in the most politically correct of manners – were no better for being able-bodied right handers, merely different).

However, I digress. The point at issue, is that in the UK, driven by the need for safety and achievement, we have learned to keep our sword hands free. And I think, it is fair to say that this precaution has long since passed into the national unconscious, if not into genetic memory.

I, of course, have spent a lifetime keeping my sword hand free. You see, it permits me to address the two primary motivators which have always driven my life. For early in childhood, right there at Mummy's knee, I learned how important it was to do what you needed to do, both to feel safe and to demonstrate achievement so as to win Mummy's approval. For never, never could you presume approval. Mummy was far too selective for that.

But now, middle age is upon me. The expiration of half a lifetime, brings me the to the point of reflection, as I guess, it does to all thinking persons. I now peer back through my bi-focals over 44 years of well-established patterns and can't help wondering, "Was this the path I was meant to choose?" What would I have been like, if I hadn't felt the need to achieve and to feel safe? You see, if you're one step ahead of me in this (and I know you often are), you will already be aware how fundamentally incompatible these two drivers really must be. Like a pendulum, they swing me in perfectly balanced dynamic equilibrium from one extreme of behaviour to the other. Today, this week, this year, I have to achieve. I must be able to demonstrate by doing better than everyone else around me that I am worth something, to somebody, somewhere. So, I choose fields of pursuit in which I know I can be competent, judiciously avoiding all of those where I have found myself to be less than excellent. And in those chosen fields, it is not enough to be as good as; I have to be better than. If there is anybody whom I am not better than, then I am inadequate. So, in my chosen fields, I soar. I rise high on eagles' wings and see the valleys spread below me. The landscape looks different from up here. You have "strategic perspective". You can see the end of the road from the beginning of the road – almost. You can see over the mountain range into the next valley where the road stretches onward, ever onward. You can almost convince yourself that if you fly high enough and far enough, you will eventually come to a place where some small sense of satisfaction might just attach itself to your soaring.

And so, you fly on, ever higher, ever further in pursuit of the unattainable; until at last you realise that a sense of achievement comes not from satisfaction with what you have done, but with satisfaction with who you are. However, herein lies the problem. It is at that point you realise that nothing you can achieve is going to make you satisfied with who you are. Then, you look around you. You see how high and how far you have flown, and you become very, very afraid. You weren't meant to fly this high. You're really incapable of flying this high. You don't have what it takes to fly this high. And as the old invidious doubts begin anew, without warning, you lose the power of flight. You plummet, panic stricken, somersaulting towards the earth. You see it rushing towards you, faster ever faster. You lose perspective. You can't see the road clearly any more, and you certainly can't see the end from the beginning. It races towards you closer, ever closer. You know you are going to crash.

And when you have crashed, you know you were wrong ever to have flown, for little boys do not have wings. Mummy was right. They only think they do. And then the most important thing is no longer to bring Mummy something that you have achieved and maybe, if she's in the right mood, win some minor acknowledgment. The most important thing now is simply to feel safe. Because the universe is not a friendly place. And it will not support you in your dreams. "Blessed is he that expecteth not … for he shall not be disappointed". Mummy taught me that; at least, she taught half of me that.

Safe means not taking risks. Safe means storing up resources, ridiculous levels of resources against some future amorphous danger. Safe means never engaging in an adventurous physical pursuit, lest you hurt yourself. And above all, safe means never ever, trying to impress Mummy in case Mummy is not impressed. Mummy is never impressed with who you are as opposed to what you do. And that is why achievement never satisfies.

I get into the car. As I turn it around on the gravel drive, I feel the stones crunch under the wheels. I press the little electronic device that causes the gates to swing open, allowing me out onto the open forest. I drive on the left of course, it keeps my sword hand free. Trouble is, though, I'm not very good with a sword in the right hand, so, I have found it is better never to engage in combat if it can possibly be avoided. And, of course, jousting for fun is a ridiculous alien notion. I am driving, late on a summer's afternoon. The sun is setting low over the horizon and at this time of day, you have to be particularly careful to avoid hitting the ponies and other creatures that graze wild on the forest. When it has been hot, they stand on the road in the shadows so as to keep cool. If you are not careful, your eyes adjust to the sun and you can't see what is in the shadows. The shadows harbour danger. I am, therefore, very, very careful when I am forced to move in the shadows.

Then, up over the hill and onto the open plain where you can see for twenty, maybe thirty miles on a clear day. Here, at the top is a place where I am told, one of the beacons stood that was lit to warn London of the impending arrival of the Spanish Armada. I stop awhile and admire the view. I need to be quiet and gather my thoughts. I pause in silent, trance-like contemplation. Shortly, I am to go down and engage in combat once again. The trouble is, that I have never fully understood the rules of engagement. It is dangerous to engage in combat when you don't know the rules; when you are sure that the other guy has an agenda, but you don't know what is. But I do know how important it is to keep my sword hand free, and to make sure that I am very, very careful when I move in the shadows.

John answers the door with his usual cheery smile. He shows me, as always, into his small study, book-lined and sporting a variety of unusual antique implements of scientific application. From the shelves his interests summon my attention. Therapeutic tomes and biographies of the greats are squeezed for breath by volumes on natural history and Buddhism. John is widely read.

We sit in our appointed places. These never change. He says there is no agenda, but some agenda items are unconscious to both of us. In the early days, my biggest problem was with not knowing what it was that, he expected of me – what his rules of engagement were. But as time wore on and we continued to meet for our regular jousts, it became increasingly evident to me, that this whole concept of there being an expectation upon me was itself an issue worthy of exploration. Why did I presuppose that there was an expectation? Because I always do. And because after so long always presupposing an expectation, it feels uncomfortable to be in an environment where there is none. There was something else that I noticed, too. There appeared to be no defined outcome. Now, I'm the kind of person that never leaves home without being certain of both destination and route, clutching directions and road atlas in my hot little hand. But here, there is no evident destination and no predefined route. Here, we appear to travel for the sake of exploration and enjoying the scenery. This is new territory. But I can take the time to enjoy it, now that I understand that we are not on a journey to anywhere. I do that in my forest all the time. So long as we are not jousting, I can enjoy. But are we jousting?

In the early days, I was very careful to keep my sword hand free and to make sure that I did not move in the shadows. There was no telling what John might do if I did not take adequate care. It seemed to me that we circled each other cautiously, each with hand on sword handle. The shadows held many dangers. And each week, as I came to psychotherapy, I would fret over not having anything to say. As I approached, my concern would be that he would simply sit and smile inquiringly, waiting for me to say something. Or, there would be that devastating introductory question "How have you been this week?" Either way, something would be expected of me. And what would happen if I got it wrong? I would experience his disapproval. And disapproval is so very, very painful. It means you are not loved. Mummy disapproved.

It took me many weeks of combat to learn that not only was there nothing expected, but also that it didn't matter if I got it wrong. Eventually, it dawned on me that it was not for John that I needed to keep my sword hand free, either. It was then, I realised who it was that I had been jousting all these years; who it was that had been standing in the shadows, precipitating my sense of danger.

It was John who introduced us. He did it with a simple question "What do you think of yourself?" I had no answer. So, he was forced to ask another: "What would somebody who likes you think of you?" (John is good at questions). And I still had no answer. Or, at least, I had no answer until I rose from the chair and strode across to the other side of the room. And from there, I could see the Shadow Man at last. He was much smaller than I had given him credit for. He carried a sword just like mine. His hand held tightly onto the handle, as did mine. Each of us was waiting for trouble. At first, we circled each other with antagonistic suspicion. It was a long, long time before either of us considered the possibility that the other might be no threat after all. But little by little, we both began to relax our grips on our sword handles.

From where I was standing I could again see a little bit more of the end from a little bit more of the beginning. Eventually, I folded my arms, stood with my feet apart, a wry smile upon my face and contemplated the Shadow Man as he looked back at me enquiringly. Somewhat to my surprise, I rather liked him. He was endearing. So, I decided to take a little time to get to know him. And you know what? He turned out to be worth knowing. As we touched and as we explored and as we found each other, I realise that he was no threat after all. In fact, you know, he had always been there; taking care of himself and maybe even taking care of me.

I don't know him very well yet. After all, we've only just been introduced. Like everybody else I know, he has some irritating habits. He's taken to waking me in the night to tell me things that I write down for him, so that he can work on them the next day. And he gets pretty cross with me if I don't do it when he wants me to. But then again, I'm sure there are some things that I do that he finds irritating too.

So, where do we go from here? Therapy's in summer recess at the moment. But right at the end of the last session John left us with a question, incisive as always (he doesn't need a sword when his questions are so sharp): "Can you love yourself?"

The Shadow Man and I, we had a problem with that one. Neither of us really had an answer at the end of that session. So, we made a bargain. We agree that we would spend the summer thinking about it. Summer is almost over. We have an answer now. We have beaten our swords into plowshares.

24. Peak Oil

Have you not heard?
The pen is mightier than the sword, they say,
mightier, sharper, dissevering deep
between a mortal's spirit and his soul.

How swiftly the embodied shed their glorious clouds,
those wispy trails of echoed godliness,
only to see them blown away upon the troposphere
where Decima writes the fate of mortals high in
blood upon the nimbus clouds.

But we are children no longer, Horatio.
So get you to your bridge,
lest Porcena's Clusian hordes
pour forth to claim the sparkling citadel.

My part for now is yet to sleep the sleep,
not of the righteous or the dead,
but of the yet unborn
while you make for me a world that you are proud
and honoured to bequeath.

And I too in my turn will call upon your name
when darkness comes
and campfire fellows call for stories of the glorious men of old.
Let not your epitaph be silence
for the shame of mighty deeds, still needful, left undone.

Roar forth those crie d'arms, man of Mars!
The noble seek for nothing more
than leave to sing of virtuous acts,
of maidens, compromised or saved,
and the long repented genocide of
Shamans reincarnate put to death.

Is it now that you would pass to me
the crystal horn
wherein mortality's elixir,
well lived and nobly sacrificed to virtue,
still dwells on?

I am come from going to and fro upon this earth of yours
and walking up and down upon it.
I have seen your world, Horatio;
a world where whitened caskets,
brim filled with hopes and the half formed dreams of nations
are carried shoulder high and laid within
sarcophagi of much loved fables once believed;
where Ideless March, a centrifuge of legends long postponed,

spins fairground horses up to Pegasean flight
and dwarfish men shave off their beards
with razor swords once honed
to sever heads of long corrupted slime-formed orcs.

Breathe on me breath of gods!
Was it in divine inebriation
you chose for this to be my time?
Your random purpose summons me to birth,
for of the many called I am the chosen;
called for my turn to walk upon the earth
chosen to hold my watch upon that unmanned bridge,
no longer with a sword and shield,
but tapping out a jolly tune upon the keyboard of an i-phone 5
while soaps flake sadly down upon a weary flickering screen.

"Peak Oil," they cry, these fearless ones and
"Give me children ere I die,"
When *"Dying is quite beyond the question, my dear,*
Being as how wanton Aphrodite stole youth s eternal fountain
right out Charmed Venus sweet hand."

Is this all you have summoned me for Horatio?
Are there no more Minotaurs to slay?
No more scaly dragons to down with a single
golden arrow from my bow,
nor even yet a serpent-headed Gorgon to decapitate?
If this is all there is, whereunto do the mighty of this age
now fall?
Where shall I find an honourable death
within a world where rich men dine on paupers
bones and drink the cellar dry?

The dragons are all gone, Horatio.
The valiant men have fallen into squabbling,
dicing for pretty rocks and beads
while all about
the unprotected die of hopelessness.

Where else but here could it have ended but here?
On sea washed golden sands under a waning
evening sun, you say?
Beside a gurgling brook within the forest glades of
soothing reassurance?
Or better yet within the golden arms of lovers long betrothed.
Oh, to reincarnate just to lie within those golden arms
and never to have heard the summons of the un-behoving.

Close your loins Horatio!
Postpone my summons yet awhile.
For I will not tread wrath's vintage
in this pestiferous cesspit
you call the Age of Reason.

Call upon me once again when you are ready to
reclaim your rotted world
and surely I will heed.
Together we will wash away the tears of wasted generations
who only ever yearned to rise on shining wings of hope.
Those admirable ghosts of lingering deities
still summon me to court
where Justice, long unblinded,

has cast aside her scaly weights
to rant affronted aphorisms
into the faces of the
whoknowswho.

Bur for this time such pens as mine are broken swords,
gestalts unchained, exhortations vilified, that sever nothing.

The clocks are running backwards, Horatio,
the superstrings unwind
and your world is falling,
falling,
spinning,
turning,
down into the vortex
of the unforgiving
Neversphere.

25. Going, Going, Gone

Going
Central London
Spring 1991

"Dr. Simpson will see you now." ("Bring in the prisoner").

The building is ancient and the room carries the echoes of a hundred years or more of medical consultation. I enter a small, bare consulting room furnished utilitarian style with desk, chairs, examination couch and a variety of instruments of torture. Nothing of consequence adorns the walls. Dr. Simpson wants to examine his patients. He does not want to touch them.

"I have the result of your tests." ("Ladies and gentlemen of the jury, have you reached a verdict?")

"I had to check that my equipment was correctly calibrated. The results were surprising". ("The prisoner will rise.")

I stand shaking in the dock awaiting sentence as judge, jury and executioner bide their time. Unconsciously, they enjoy the sense of control that the withholding of the verdict bestows upon them.

"The equipment was correctly calibrated" ("We have My Lord.")

"You have a hearing loss at speech frequencies; 25% on the left and 40% on the right." ("The prisoner is guilty.")

I concentrate very hard, trying to take in both facts and implications of facts. 25%. That's not a lot. That shouldn't make much difference to me. I'll still be able to work.

I begin to make meaning out of the information I am being given. And then the questions start to flow. I suppress the panic.

"Do you have any questions?" ("Does the prisoner have anything to say?")

"Will this deterioration continue?" ("I have nothing to say in my defence, My Lord.")

"I am unable to tell you". ("Then I sentence you to be detained at Her Majesty's pleasure").

"So, what do I do now?"("I can't take this in... Make a decision for me... Tell me what the hell to do.")

"I'm going to give you the name of a company, close by here, that can help you. They make hearing aids. You can go right there now, if you want to." ("Remove the prisoner from the dock. Take him down").

"Here's where to find them." ("Next Case.")

He scribbles an address on a scrap of paper and hands it to me. ("It is not my problem anymore, so get out and let me see my next patient. My secretary will send you a bill — the very biggest bill we can possibly justify and then some. We're unlikely to see you again anyway, so frankly my dear, we don't given a damn.")

I extricate myself from the soulless consulting room, dazed and confused. If I had been the victim of a crime, if I had been the perpetrator of a crime, then, the well-oiled machinery of the social system would have spun noiselessly into action. Somebody, somewhere would have taken responsibility. But now, as I leave the building, pulling the shiny black door closed behind me by its brass handle, and step down into Harley Street, the traffic seems somehow quieter. There is only me.

There are too many unanswered questions and no one to put them to. Oh sure, somebody, somewhere is going to sell me a piece of equipment. Somebody, somewhere is going to talk to me about the technical aspects of hearing deterioration. Somebody, somewhere is going to be pleased to demonstrate their competence in a technical field I do not yet understand. Somebody, somewhere is going to be delighted to take a fat cheque from me in order to help me sit upon my throne, Canute-like on the beach, as I command the approaching waves to retreat.

But nobody, anywhere, is actually going to want to tell me what is going to be like to go deaf. And so, I will conjure my reality, as always, from the innumerable memories of childhood and beyond, that now crowd upon my consciousness. For we are meaning-making creatures, and we must rationalise our circumstances. We seek to define a purposeful universe and to identify reasons for the random events that happen to us. We can cope with the spin of the roulette wheel in the casino but we cannot relate to randomness in our day-to-day lives. For that, of course, would imply that we are out of control. And masters of the universe cannot possibly be out of control.

There comes to mind only the old man who lived next-door. I was eight years old. He was a thousand years old. He leaned across the fence and smiled his toothless smile. I was afraid. He could not make me feel safe. He wore plastic on his ears and couldn't understand me when I spoke. I did not like him. My daddy liked him. He tried to talk to him. But the old man couldn't hear, so even daddy gave up eventually. And my childhood eyes saw sadness that I absorbed, but could not articulate.

Now, I am a thousand years old. I will lean across the divide. I will try to talk to you. And at first, you will try to talk to me; but you will give up because the plastic on my ears will stop me hearing you. Or, perhaps, it is I, who will give up because I think that/you think the plastic on my ears will stop me hearing you. And all I will be left with is my toothless smile, which I will beam at you because I shall have no other way of touching you. You will be afraid, and I will not be able to make you feel safe.

And now, begins the process, the painful step-by-step realisation, that nothing is ever going to be the same again. At the technical level, I am fitted with a hearing aid. It is small enough to fit inside my ear. That pleases me. The device's invisibility means I can convince you for a little longer that I am not deaf. And if I can convince you, maybe, just maybe, I can convince myself. And if I can convince myself, maybe, just maybe, it is not going to happen.

Yet, it is not at the technical level, but at the emotional where we find our equilibrium. Here, we make the adjustments to the changes in external reality that beat upon the windows and doors of our perception. They force their way, unbidden, into our private places. And there, they make themselves at home. They sit themselves down and invite themselves to tea as if they had every right to take possession of the comfort zones which we have created for ourselves. And it is then, that we begin to realise that we must provide living space to the unbidden house guests of reality that refused to retire.

Thus, at first, unconsciously, the redrawing of strategies

begins. Work requires very little change from me. I merely have to make my clients aware that I am "just a little hard of hearing," and watch for the minute changes in body language that will identify to me whether they are prepared to accommodate the smallest of disabilities. Some do, some don't. And for those that don't, it is not a difficult task to convince myself, I didn't really want that assignment anyway. You are not my kind of person. I don't like to work with people who can't make reasonable space for the needs of others. I can pretend quite easily in the context of work that my identity is unaffected by your attitude. But there again, if you make a special effort because you have dealt with the hearing-impaired before, and if you understand that it does not affect my competence as a management consultant, then, I will warm especially towards you. I will want to call you "friend". Even if you don't really want to be called friend, you are nevertheless my friend. And I will work that much harder to generate for you the special result I want to give you.

Regrettably though, many of our communications are not deep and carefully considered. A lot consist of the fleeting interactions that we make with others as we go about our daily business. And here, because we think the people whose paths we cross do not really matter to us, we are apt to make far fewer allowances for one another. We tend to position people we do not know as walking shadows, poor players who strut and fret their hour upon a stage that is irrelevant to us. They are meaningless spectres, full of sound and fury with no consequence to our real lives. So, it is here in this context that the pain begins.

The real problem with deafness is its inherently invisible nature. Were I in a wheel chair, were I to have a club foot, you would see my disability. I might not like your reaction, but you would know, and you would reposition your responses accordingly. Because deafness is invisible, it is different. I have to learn not to touch you. And I have to learn that you will presume that I am as you – that I communicate as you do – that I hear as you hear. Are your presumptions reasonable? We all make them, don't we? We all assume that what is going on for us is the same as what is going on for the other person. And when, for some small reason our worlds collide, and we do not get the response we want or expect, we call one another "fool", or "prejudiced", or "ignorant", or make one of innumerable other judgments that allow us to maintain our unique sense of individuality from a map of the world we just know instinctively is right. We will rarely allow another sufficiently far past the veneer to redefine our prejudices for us.

Going
Suburban London
Summer 1997

I have learned not to make eye contact. For eye contact will lead inevitably to the intricate dance of minor social interaction where you want to tell me how mother's bunions are, or to comment on the weather we've been having. The danger here is, I will miss something that you say, and thus, misinterpret the sense you seek to convey. If I have misunderstood, then, I may reply in some unacceptable form, and that will be incongruent. We do not like incongruence, for it forces us to confront the fact that others navigate from maps of the world that differ from our own. And depending on who you are, depending on how polite mother taught you to be, you will think me fool; you will call me fool… or worse.

I have also learned there are situations that are not safe for me. And that which is not safe is to be judiciously avoided. So, I don't go to your cocktail parties anymore, lest you seek to make small talk with me. And, I don't accept invitations to your dinner parties anymore, lest you sit me next somebody who will not make allowances, and who will think me fool. And before I enter into any one a hundred different social interactions, I take my life in my hands and wonder if there will be pain. More often than not, the value of the contact, since the conversation is usually mere chaff, is not enough to make me want to take the risk. Thus, I make some unconvincing excuse and back off from contact. I do not do chaff easily.

The places that are safest are the places I know well. The people that are safest are the people I know well. But sometimes, I have to step out of the safety zone. Sometimes… a lot of times, there is just no alternative.

Each week, like you, I pushed the trolley round the supermarket. Unlike you, I do not buy at the deli counter because that means talking to someone and unnecessary communication is best avoided. But just like you, I have to pay the checkout girls.

And checkout girls hunt in packs.

They place themselves strategically at the ends of the aisles, between their chosen victims and the exit, so that there is no escape. And now, I live in fear of meeting the Alpha female again. For, once upon a time, we did meet. She spoke, and I did not hear. So, my response was inappropriate, incongruent. And because my behaviour was not consistent with her map of the world, I was fool. The Alpha female knows how to hunt. She circles cautiously to reassure herself you are no threat. The relaxed, lazy rippling of her muscles make you think you just might be able to escape. But the moment you let down your guard, she lunges for your jugular. While you grip your throat so as not to let your lifeblood spill all over the nice clean supermarket floor, she rips your heart from your rib cage. And the rest of the pack howls their approval of her hunting prowess.

Checkout girls enjoy the kill. It is the most exciting part of the hunt.

I died that day. Or, if not all of me, some part of me that is no longer there. Now, I am in awe of the Alpha female. I do my shopping on the internet. And should need arise to step out of cyberspace and into a real supermarket, then I check carefully, for I must ensure that she is hunting elsewhere, toying with some other prey; lest she again choose to tear my heart from me. Then the supermarket cleaners would have to mop blood from the floor.

Cleaners do not like blood.

**Going
The Forest
Autumn 1999**

"Dr Abbot will see you now." ("I declare this review board open.")

With an overwhelming sense of déjà vu, I enter another consulting room. The building is again ancient and the room carries the echoes of a hundred years or more of medical consultation. The instruments of torture are familiar. But the environment is not as soulless as before. The chairs are comfortable; the pictures on the wall speak of Englishness – warm beer in the sunshine and cricket on a summer's day. Look at them long enough and you can hear the crack of willow on leather – if you can hear such things, that is.

This time the face is human. (Perhaps there will be a reprieve. Review board chairmen only smile if there's going to be a reprieve).

"I have the results of your test."("Ladies and gentlemen of the review board have you reached a decision?")

"The results were not surprising." ("Please stand.")

"Your hearing has continued to deteriorate. At speech frequencies you have lost 60% on the left and 80% on the right." ("It is our considered opinion that there should be no reprieve.")

I concentrate very hard, trying to take in both facts and the implications of facts. 80% deterioration. That is a lot. I will not be able to work. At least, I will not be able to do the work I am used to doing. No one wants a deaf consultant.

I begin to make meaning out of the information. There is no panic to suppress. You cannot panic at the inevitable. The questions do not flow. There is only one.

"Will this deterioration continue?" ("Can I make another appeal later?")

"I rather think it probably will." ("Your sentence is confirmed. You will be incarcerated for the rest of your natural life.")

"Think of it this way. Imagine everybody is born with one million hair cells on the cochlea. During the course of our lives it is natural for them to atrophy. You have a genetic disorder. You were born with fewer. Yours atrophy faster." ("I'm really very sorry. I really do care.")

I thank the nice doctor for his help.

I extricate myself from the consulting room.

My mind is clear.

I leave the building, pulling the shiny black door closed behind me by its brass handle.

I step down into the traffic free street of the small Forest town.

There is only me.

Going
The Forest
Summer 2000

It hasn't been much of a summer. The temperatures have been low, the sunshine limited, the rain copious. Nevertheless, we are going to have a pool party. I don't really do parties for all the reasons you already know. But if there is a safe party, it is my own party; because no one is going to call me fool in my own home. And anyway, friends are coming and friends are safe. In particular, Susan is coming. Susan is a social worker for the deaf. And social workers do not hunt in packs. Everybody bullshits me about my hearing. Susan does not. She speaks honestly and talks directly. I prefer that.

She comes round the corner of the house, relaxed as always, soft smile upon her face, friendly husband in tow. I am safe. I need to talk to Susan. I need to tell her the verdict and I need her help. And when I do, she is straight with me as always.

"I cannot tell you how long you will be able to work, but I know the time is coming when you will not be able to do the kind of work that you do now. The deterioration will continue. And when the right time comes, I will recommend to you a variety of solutions that will make life easier. But you have to understand that all hearing aids merely amplify the hearing that you have. And when that is gone, nothing can compensate. You have to adjust."

Susan does not bullshit me. Social workers do not enjoy the

kill. They hunt alone and kill humanely. I prefer that. It minimises the blood on the floor. I die again. It's my party and I'll die if I want to.

Gone
The Forest
An unspecified future date

Summer has turned to winter. Snow carpets the forest floor. It is silent.

Reach across the wall to me, my brother, even as I am reaching across to you now. It is a pleasure for me to reach half way, but I cannot touch you unless you, too, stretch out your hand. If you are willing, we can hold each other across the boundary that divides your world of tumult from my world of peace.

This wall is of your making, not of mine. Allow me to reach your hand, and together, we shall breech it. Allow me to touch your soul and I will make you this promise: together we are capable of tearing down this barrier between us. And in so doing, you shall relieve yourself of your disability – the very prejudice that prevents you from perceiving who I am and receiving what I have to offer.

Do not feel sorry for me in the silence, my sister. Rather, permit yourself to conceive of the possibility that I may more appropriately be envied than pitied. I am, who I am for cause of the roads I have trodden. I would not be who I am, I would not have learned what I have learned and thus, be able to offer you what I do offer, without the growing silence that has come to be my world.

Do you consider my inability to hear to be a disability? It is not. I am disabled, not by the silence, but rather, by your attitude to the silence. You disable me by your presumption that since I look as you look, I must hear as you hear. You disable me by your unwillingness to provide me with the technology that already exists which would allow me to communicate with you. You disable me when you refuse to subtitle your television programmes. You disable me when you do not turn on the induction loops in your cinemas and theatres, causing me public humiliation when I am forced to ask you to do so. You disable me when you speak at your preferred volume with your preferred degree of clarity. You disable me by the embarrassment in which you look away from me when you realise I cannot hear you. You consider these to be my disabilities? They are not my disabilities. They are yours.

Take my hand, my brother, my sister. Take my hand and look into my eyes. Then, without breaking from the gaze we hold together, reach down and take a brick from the wall. Cast it to the ground and as it shatters, smile into my eyes. For at last, we touch, soul to soul.

26. Before Abraham

I am darkness
I am light
burning day and blackened night.
I am laughter
I am pain
I am sunshine
I am rain.
I am force unleashed in power,
I am the Tao within the flower.
I am spirit,
I am essence,
solid rock and effervescence,
unbound strength and burning fire,
satiate, yet raw desire,
deluging my energy
to integrate in synergy.

Am I loss or am I gain?
Open-eyed, do not constrain
the essence of my will to be:
all around you – this is me.

Earth will ground and air is still,
fires consume and waters fill.
The substance of identity:
wholly you, yet wholly me.
Lose yourself in holding fast
I am your first, I am your last.
Imbibe my being, touch my soul,
infuse my essence – be made whole.
Look in my eyes, begin to see
releasing "I" makes way for "we."

We wind ourselves in spirit light
and burn on still where dark is bright,
by virtue of such energy
where is no mass or entropy.
We are divine
and we are man
preceding time when time began.
Coming going, lifetimes pass,
we peer into the looking glass
where eye meets eye and heart meets heart
we have no end, we have no start.
We have been and always will,
we inhale time, hold motion still.
We pass beyond this roaring sea,
embracing immortality.

Here Sons of Grace and Reprobate
return to Source at heaven's gate.
Here mighty men relinquish power,
confronted at their witching hour.
Here notions cease and tongues are spent.

Desire yields enlightenment.
Emotions wane and fade from sight,
discarded in the burning light.

When all is done we surely know
there is no come, there is no go.
Conjoined below, infused above,
when all is ended…
We are Love

27. Heart's Home

Here is a road that anyone can tread. I have set foot upon the journey many times before, but alas, I am so easily distracted. So few will take the risk of travelling at all. But now, I have met you. You seek to be a traveller, as I seek to be a traveller. And here, together, we have stumbled upon the way. Now we can begin, falteringly at first, to lead each other to places we have never been before. Here, it is good for the blind to lead the blind; for we shall be thrown upon the mercy of revelations, having not the power of sight. Now, we have set out, we know that we can never turn back by choice. How can you retrace your steps when the deeps within you whisper perpetually, confidently, that you have finally found the way home? So now, we hunger and thirst to reach the place where souls touch. Our hearts have been awakened.

We, so easily silence our hearts, don't we? They would talk to us of the deep places where men and women are meant to live. They would guide us in the ways of eternity and spirit growth. But we allow ourselves instead to be distracted from what they have to say.. We pour sleeping potions into their coffee so that we can afford pride of place to concerns of the day. Getting it and spending it; beginning it and ending it, we de-alchemise and gaily turn gold into lead.

We do not notice the lead at first, for there is only a little extra weight to carry – an ounce or two here, the odd ingot there. But the white hot fire of the ego melts it. Like obesity, it creeps and spreads until it surrounds the heart. And hearts cannot be heard through lead. They cry for us to listen but the plombe siren song of the comfort zone wraps them, muffles them. A car would be cool. A big house will be nice. A week on the beach is well within reach. A degree will define my destiny. We devote our time to polishing our egos. Then, before we realise what has happened, the heart has been silenced. Soon, if there is no intervention it will lie unheeded until it is too late.

But if we are really fortunate, something happens to wake us before we pass the point of no return. Something warms the soul enough – or maybe something cools it enough – to make us realise we are closer to midnight than we thought. Then, the lead is riven, and the heart is heard again. "Now or never," is its cry. "Let me breathe within you. Let me dance to the choreography of the spheres. I must do that for which I was made. I hunger to touch, to unite deep unto deep. I have a lifetime of tears that I must add to the river of life that flows from eternity to eternity."

And thus, confronted, will we act? The decision is difficult for us. Spiritual awareness never comes conveniently shrink-wrapped in individual sized portions. We cannot slice ourselves a big enough piece for one day, then, pop the rest in the freezer to keep for later. Hearts don't grow if you freeze them.

But there's always something else to do, isn't there? There's always something more immediate, though never more important. If we ignore the cry for just a little longer perhaps, we can pretend we never heard it at all. We can continue to convince ourselves that life is made of bigger bucks and Cadillacs, business deals and faster wheels, getting it and spending it, beginning it and ending it – until they lay us in the cold, silent earth; silent, as we have silenced our hearts within us for so very, very long. And silence then will be our eulogy.

So, will the silenced heart be our whole history? Will they write upon our tombstone "Here lies one who covered his ears to muffle the voice within?" And will this be our obituary: He dealt another dollar. He traded another trinket. He discharged another ill-considered, self-imposed obligation that kept him busy, busy, busy and so safe from that most incisive of all questions:

> *"Whereunto was I born? What*
> *is the purpose of my being?"*

STOP!

Sit there and listen. And, as you listen, give up your certainties and shibboleths that now the questions might begin to flow. And if you're charmed enough or quiet enough to hear the questions, whatever you do, don't try to answer them. Answers bring closure and closure is ending. We travellers seek openings, learning, beginnings. We want to expand, ever to increase, ever to grow. Leave behind the certainties of "right and wrong," "is and is not," "yes and no." Take time to wallow in the uncertainty of "may be" and "could be". Luxuriate in the state of not knowing and glorious, glorious confusion. For herein lies the beginning of wisdom.

There are many changes we will need to make, now we

have chosen this path. Much must be unlearned, for learning of the mind has served its purpose and had its season. All those nice, impenetrable building blocks that we have carefully crafted into that lovely, cosy castle have now to be dismantled. There are pinnacles of pride to be demolished, drawbridges of desensitisation to be torn down; moats of self-satisfaction to be drained. It is time for deconstruction if we truly want to go forward; if we really want to grow; if we hunger to know as we are known.

For, when question has begat question for eons enough, that finally, we understand the purpose of questions, then, we may just be ready for the greatest challenge yet. Then, and only then, we burst with excitement and our soul soars back to the heavens from which we came. There, all the metaphors we have learned to treat as truth incarnate through all the years of illusion-life merge into a single Damascene revelation. The scales fall from our eyes.

All the begetting and the birthing; all the generations upon generations of humankind adding to the birth cry of the universe, are rising to the heights of ecstasy in inexorable, irresistible, axiomatic, avataristic revelation.

Now, I see! Now, I know! Here I know as I am known! He; she; it; they. Use your favoured name. God; Allah; Shiva; Tao. The endless stream of words that we have used to name the unnameable pass now into uselessness, unneeded and unheeded. Here, words are superfluous. Here, we are held in the arms of that, which was, and is, and is to come. Here is a place beyond our mental comprehension.

Here is heart's home.

28. Within a World

And hast thou heard
how by his word
God, in their courses, did the planets set?
And hast thou seen,
as in a dream
By this, thy deepest longings, he has met?
Then know, thou soul,
this is the whole:
eternity, infinity begets;
and by thy word
the truth preferred
by thee, and courses of thy life are set.

If thou dost speak,
what thou dost seek
here in thy flesh is brought to be.
And if thy heart
will from the start
seek now to make its own reality,
worlds of thine own,
by faith alone,

set forth before thee thou shalt surely see.
In congruence
and elegance
thine own desires become an entity.

Thou dost believe,
and wilt perceive
reality, immutable, is set.
By this device
through thine own choice
thy yearning for security is met.
But take to thee
maturity –
simplistic notions of thy youth forget.
Now rather see
complexity
will here a new reality beget.

Thy world of youth,
once held as truth,
around thee now comes crashing down.
Volcanoes flow
and Hell below
thy soul, with sulph'rous brimstone, here doth pound.
Now wouldst thou hold
in terror cold
the pillars of thy former faith unsound.
For thou dost find
within thy mind
foundation rock has turned to quicksand ground.

Eventually,
thou com'st to see
the weakness of thy former argument,
and thus begin
to form within
a new belief thou tak'st as heaven-sent;
foundations lay
within thy way
and so the earlier truth will now repent –
instead believe
and do perceive
a new philosophy makes thee content.

So here and now
thy soul doth vow
a new conception of reality
to seek and find.
Within thy mind
parameters of faith now shift to be
new paradigm.
Within its time
a new-held constant of veracity
is thine to hold
to be the mould
for faith, and of spirituality.

From time to time
thou look'st behind
and backward glance occasionally make –
disdaining youth
and former truth
and patronize beliefs as a mistake.

Self-satisfied
thou dost deride
thy former ignorance. For pity's sake!
Despise no more
what came before
and necessary learning thus forsake.

For thou has come
and hast begun
to climb a little higher in thy heart.
But this can be
the path for thee
because it was in ignorance thou made'st a start.
Now thou art more
than wert before -
of spiritual growth can take a part.
Acknowledge now
the hand of Tao
and honour still the ways thou did'st depart.

The time passed by.
The years did fly,
and comf'table within thy patterns thou became.
And gradually
thine energy
and passion for more truth began to wane.
Thy vision slept.
Thy soul, once kept
in fiery faith, now sadly doused its inner flame.
And comf'table,
intractable
thy former heart of passion thus became.

And now thy world
once more is hurled
to turmoil's epicentre here.
The fires now rain.
thy heart, in pain,
screams for security, and it is clear
now unto thee
that there will be
no respite from the terror thou dost fear
'til thou begin
to sense within
that change and growth are paths that call thee here.

So learn, thou soul,
this is the whole:
God's grace forever on thy heart doth lie.
When tempests come
and freeze the sun
then put to Heaven not the question "Why?"
Change sets us free
from constancy
and plagues of comfort on which we rely.
Thy calling's now
to rise and go –
to learn and grow in grace until you die.

Come angel band!
Now take my hand
and pour thy revelations through this pen.
Come inner world
within a world
and smite within me now the ways of men.

The erudite
now set to flight
the vacuous, urbane and vapid then
put to the sword
of Heaven's word.
My education now begin again!

Biographical

Michael Forester is a deafened writer who lives in Hampshire's New Forest with his hearing dog, Matt.

He can be contacted at michaelforesterauthor@gmail.com

Michael Forester with hearing dog Matt